Fodor's

hong kong

first edition

Excerpted from Fodor's Hong Kong
fodor's travel publications
new york · toronto · london · sydney · auckland
www.fodors.com

contents

	on the road with fodor's	iv
	Don't Forget to Write v	
📖	introducing hong kong	2
🚏	here and there	8
✕	eating out	38
🛍	shopping	62
🍸	nightlife and the arts	90
🏨	where to stay	100
💡	practical information	122
📖	index	148

maps

hong kong island 10

hong kong mass transit railway 11

central and western districts 16–17

wanchai, causeway bay, happy valley, and north point 24–25

kowloon 34

dining 42–43

kowloon dining 58

lodging 104–105

kowloon lodging 111

on the road with fodor's

THE MORE YOU KNOW BEFORE YOU GO, the better your trip will be. Hong Kong's most fascinating small museum or its most innovative fish house could be just around the corner from your hotel, but if you don't know it's there, it might as well be across the globe. That's where this guidebook and our Web site, Fodors.com, come in. Our editors work hard to give you useful, on-target information. Their efforts begin with finding the best contributors—people with good judgment and broad travel experience—the people you'd poll for tips yourself if you knew them.

Hong Kong native **Denise Cheung** has combined a career in journalism with a taste for travel. Particularly enamored of Hong Kong's booming restaurant scene, she has written for a number of publications, including the South China Morning Post and HK magazine about food and lifestyle. She updated the Eating Out chapter.

Born in Hong Kong and raised in Australia, **Eva Chui** returned to her birthplace in 1995. She has worked as entertainment editor for HK magazine and as a producer for Channel V, Asia's No.1 music-TV station. Currently, she divides her time between writing and working in the television and film industries in Hong Kong. Eva updated the Nightlife and the Arts chapter in this book.

British native **Tobias Parker,** who updated the Where to Stay chapter for this edition, arrived in Hong Kong in 1996 shortly before his government's departure. After renouncing the world of print publishing, where he was an editor and journalist for a number of books and magazines, he became content manager for the Hong Kong Tourist Board's Web site, where he developed the successful weekly, *Hong Kong This Week*.

Lara Wozniak, a Hong Kong resident for many years, is a U.S. lawyer and an assistant editor for the *Far Eastern Economic Review*, a daily English-language newspaper in Hong Kong. She regularly contributes to American, Canadian, and British newspapers and magazines. She wrote the Nepal chapter for the *Fodor's Nepal, Tibet, and Bhutan, 1st edition,* and updated the Practical Information and Shopping chapters for this edition.

We'd also like to thank the Hong Kong Tourism Board for their help in preparing this edition.

Don't Forget to Write

Keeping a travel guide fresh and up-to-date is a big job. So we love your feedback—positive and negative—and follow up on all your suggestions. Contact the Pocket Hong Kong editor at editors@fodors.com or c/o Fodor's, 280 Park Avenue, New York, New York 10017. And have a wonderful trip!

Karen Cure
Editorial Director

hong kong

In This Chapter

Quick Tours 5

introducing hong kong

CANTONESE FOR "FRAGRANT HARBOR," the name Hong Kong refers to the areas of the New Territories (not covered in this book) and Kowloon, as well Hong Kong Island. Hong Kong is 98% Chinese. Although the territory's official languages are English and Cantonese, the use of Mandarin (or *Putonghua*), China's official language, is on the rise. Other languages and dialects include Hakka, Tanka, and Shanghainese. Some 150,000 Filipinos make up the largest foreign community; most are women working as maids and nannies (amahs in local parlance).

The three great strands of Chinese thought—Buddhism, Taoism, and Confucianism—together with Christianity make up Hong Kong's major religions, and you'll see signs of them everywhere. Chinese people tend toward eclecticism in their beliefs, so the distinctions between faiths are often blurred.

Hong Kong's earliest visitors are believed to have been people of Malaysian-Oceanic origin who arrived by boat about 5,000 years ago. More than 600 years later, the Tang Dynasty left lime kilns full of seashells. In the 13th century, Sung Dynasty loyalists fled China with their child emperor to escape the invading Mongols. The boy was the only Chinese emperor believed to have set foot in what is now Hong Kong. One of his men is credited with naming Kowloon, which means "nine dragons" (he counted eight mountain peaks that resembled dragons and added one for the emperor, who was also considered a dragon).

Western traders first appeared in the Hong Kong area in 1513. The first were Portuguese, but they were soon followed by the Spanish, Dutch, English, and French. All were bent on making fortunes trading porcelain, tea, and silk. China wanted nothing from the West except silver, until the British started offering opium.

As early as 1729, Chinese officials issued edicts forbidding importation of opium, but these rules were regularly circumvented. The tension between the government and foreign traders led to the Opium Wars and a succession of treaties enforced by superior British firepower. The most important of these required China to cede Kowloon and the island of Hong Kong to Britain. In 1898, China leased the New Territories to Britain for 99 years—it was the expiration of this lease that led to the handover of Hong Kong to China in 1997.

The handover seems anticlimactic in hindsight. For most Hong Kongers, business takes precedence over all other issues and it was the Asian crisis, which hit within a month of the handover, that became the real news of 1997 and the years that followed. The side effects were high interest rates and high inflation, making Hong Kong one of the most expensive places in the world to live and do business.

But for all the uncertain moments, the SAR pulled through, and with the stock market soaring it is easy to forget the economy was ever imperiled. Indeed, except for a few other small differences, the changes wrought by the handover are mostly ones of increasing integration between the local and mainland economies, a process that has been under way for at least two decades. Culturally, ties have been strengthened since Hong Kong's terrestrial TV stations have been received in south China, displaying Hong Kong's lifestyle for all to see.

Perhaps the greatest sign that Hong Kong is operating quite comfortably under Chinese rule is that political debate has, for the most part, centered on issues like pollution rather than the much-feared crackdown on individual liberty. Graves are still swept on the Ching Ming and Chung Yeung holidays. The Buddha's birthday has been added to the official holiday list but the four-day Easter weekend and the two-day Christmas–Boxing Day respite remain on the calendar as well. The local press, though subject to some self-censorship, still thrives; international reporting, publishing, and broadcasting continue unabated. Great debates rage in the local print and electronic media, and everyone has time to check up on the stock market.

—By Jan Alexander and Saul Lockhart; updated by Eva Chui

QUICK TOURS

Each tour is designed to take one day. See Here and There for more information on individual sights.

HONG KONG ISLAND TOUR

Start with a trip to the top of **Victoria Peak** by taking the **Peak Tram,** the steepest funicular railway in the world. From here you can get a bird's-eye view of Central's sparkling high-rises, the densely packed streets of Hong Kong Island, the harbor, and all the way to the outer edges of Kowloon. Descend back into **Central** and spend the rest of your day checking out the centers of activity on Hong Kong Island: the harbor districts of **Central** and **Western** with their upscale shopping and landmark skyscrapers, the **Midlevels** with its series of outdoor escalators leading up the steep mountainside, the hustling **Wanchai** district, and **Causeway Bay** and **Admiralty** with their megamalls and department stores. If you finish up your day in Admiralty, consider getting dinner at one of the great restaurants in the Pacific Place shopping complex.

Your checklist for a perfect journey

WAY AHEAD
- Devise a trip budget.
- Write down the five things you want most from this trip. Keep this list handy before and during your trip.
- Make plane or train reservations. Book lodging and rental cars.
- Arrange for pet care.
- Check your passport. Apply for a new one if necessary.
- Photocopy important documents and store in a safe place.

A MONTH BEFORE
- Make restaurant reservations and buy theater and concert tickets. Visit fodors.com for links to local events.
- Familiarize yourself with the local language or lingo.

TWO WEEKS BEFORE
- Replenish your supply of medications.
- Create your itinerary.
- Enjoy a book or movie set in your destination to get you in the mood.
- Develop a packing list. Shop for missing essentials. Repair and launder or dry-clean your clothes.

A WEEK BEFORE
- Stop newspaper deliveries. Pay bills.
- Acquire traveler's checks.
- Stock up on film.
- Label your luggage.
- Finalize your packing list— take less than you think you need.
- Create a toiletries kit filled with travel-size essentials.
- Get lots of sleep. Don't get sick before your trip.

A DAY BEFORE
- Drink plenty of water.
- Check your travel documents.
- Get packing!

DURING YOUR TRIP
- Keep a journal/scrapbook.
- Spend time with locals.
- Take time to explore. Don't plan too much.

KOWLOON TOUR

If you're staying on Hong Kong Island, take a ride on the **Star Ferry** to arrive in the **Tsim Sha Tsui** neighborhood at the tip of Kowloon (if you're staying in Kowloon, use the ferry to arrive on Hong Kong Island for the Hong Kong Island Tour). The view of the towering city from the water is always an impressive one. Not far from the **Star Ferry Terminal** are the Hong Kong Space, Science, Art, and History museums. Farther along Nathan Road is the **Peninsula Hotel,** one of the true landmarks of Hong Kong. Take a peek at the palatial lobby, stop in for a cup of coffee, or come back later for the justifiably popular afternoon high tea. Continue up **Nathan Road,** crammed with stores big and small, on your way to the temples of **Tin Hau,** the oldest in Hong Kong, and **Wong Tai Sin,** an explosively colorful and noisy spot with a full concourse of fortune tellers. Also take this opportunity to visit some of the diverse markets that are unique to Hong Kong. The **Bird Garden,** with birdcages lining the walkways and busy vendors selling cricket treats for their beloved songbird pets, particularly stands out. Other markets in the area include the enclosed **Jade Market,** the **Flower Market** (most interesting in the time leading up to the New Year), and the **Ladies Market** and **Night Market** (the latter starts around 6 PM). Wrap up your day in Kowloon with a drink or dinner at the Peninsula's **Felix** restaurant for unparalleled views of neon-lit Central.

In This Chapter

HONG KONG ISLAND 9 • Central and Western Districts 9 • From Central to the Peak 21 • Wanchai 23 • Causeway Bay, Happy Valley, and North Point 26 • South Side 29 • KOWLOON 32

Updated by Eva Chui

here and there

IT'S HARD TO BELIEVE that almost everything you see in Hong Kong was built in the time since today's young investment bankers were born. And it can be easy to forget that most of Hong Kong has nothing to do with business or skyscrapers: three-quarters of it is actually rural land and wilderness. So whether you're looking for the hectic Hong Kong or the relaxed one, both are easy enough to find—indeed, sometimes only a few minutes apart.

All museums offer free admission on Wednesday. The Hong Kong Tourism Board (HKTB) offers a Museum Tour pass for HK$50, good for the Museum of Art and Space, Science, History, and Heritage museums. The pass includes a shuttle bus to each location.

HONG KONG ISLAND

With everything from high finance to nightlife to luxury shopping at their fingertips, many residents feel little reason to ever leave the 77 square-km (30 square-mi) island of Hong Kong. The island has few historic landmarks (largely because soaring property values have caused older buildings to be torn down and replaced), but it pulses with a dynamic contemporary life.

CENTRAL AND WESTERN DISTRICTS

Central houses nearly every major investment and commercial bank, fashion designer, and luxury-goods boutique the world

hong kong island

has yet produced. The streets are often so crowded with bankers and shoppers that a pedestrian feels like a fish swimming upstream. On Sunday, many Central shops close and the district teems with thousands of maids who spend their day off in the public gardens, sidewalks, and plazas.

The Western district is gradually becoming more like Central, but it still retains a traditional feel. Most of the buildings are highrises, but in some of the small alleys off Western's main streets, the old China Coast comes alive. Traditional shops sell curled

hong kong mass transit railway

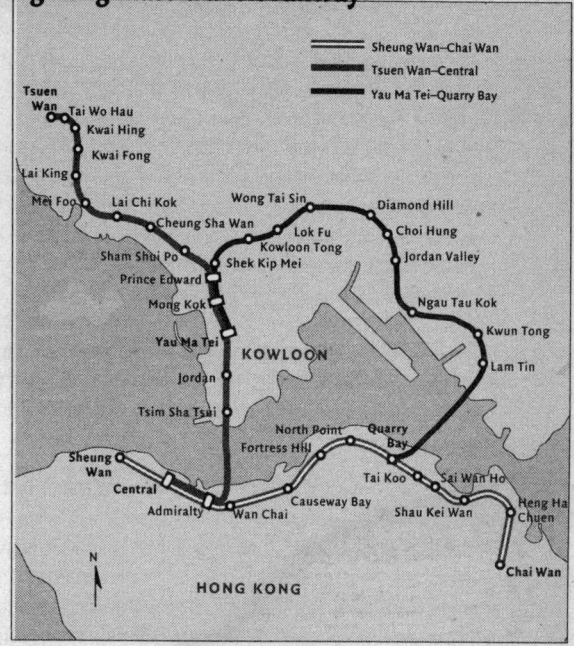

snakes, salted fish, aromatic mushrooms, herbal medicines, and, of course, tea.

Numbers in the text correspond to numbers in the margin and on the Central and Western Districts map.

A Good Walk

Walking is by far the best way to get around Central and Western, and orientation is easy since the harbor is always north. Start at the **STAR FERRY TERMINAL** ①. To your right is the General Post Office, and behind it is the towering **JARDINE HOUSE** ② with its many round windows. Follow the awnings to the right and go through the underground walkway to **STATUE SQUARE** ③. The intriguing Victorian–Chinese hybrid building on the east side of the square is the **LEGISLATIVE COUNCIL BUILDING** ④. Along the southern end of the square are the buildings of Hong Kong's three note-issuing banks: the former **BANK OF CHINA** ⑤ headquarters, the spectacular strut-and-ladder facade of the **HONGKONG & SHANGHAI BANK (HSBC)** ⑥, and, pressing up against it, the rose-color wedge of Standard Chartered Bank. Exiting HSBC on the south side, cross the street (Queen's Road Central) and turn left past the giant Cheung Kong building (on your right) and Chater Garden (on your left) until you come to the triangle-scheme Bank of China Tower, with its adjacent Chinese waterfall garden.

Head back on Queen's Road Central toward HSBC and walk until you get to the intersection with Pedder Street, where you'll find **THE LANDMARK** ⑦, the mother of all luxury shopping centers. Exit and turn left (south) on Pedder Street and walk straight up the steep hill until you pass the colonial red-and-white-striped building on the left that hosts the Fringe Club, an avant-garde arts center. At the five-street intersection, a sharp right takes you into Lan Kwai Fong, a prime entertainment district, but veering right gets you to **WYNDHAM STREET** ⑧ and the start of a breathtaking series of antiques and Oriental-rug galleries. At the old Central Police Station, Wyndham Street turns into Hollywood Road, and you'll see an overpass that forms a link in the open-air **MIDLEVELS ESCALATOR** ⑨. Join up with it by turning left up an incline; once aboard, take it all the way up the hill until you see an elaborate metalwork gate on the left. The gate hides a small garden and the tranquil **JAMIA MOSQUE** ⑩, built in 1915.

Follow the escalator back downhill to **HOLLYWOOD ROAD** ⑪, perhaps stopping for a meal in the hip Elgins and Staunton Street areas en route. Turn left on Hollywood Road and follow the antiques shops to the colorful **MAN MO TEMPLE** ⑫. To reach the curio and trinket shops of **UPPER LASCAR ROW** ⑬ (also known as Cat Street), walk down the steps of Ladder Street, just across from Man Mo Temple. Continue down to **QUEEN'S ROAD CENTRAL** ⑭ and turn left (west) to see a bit of the old Hong Kong that may otherwise seem to have disappeared. Turn right on Cleverly Street, then left. Both **BONHAM STRAND EAST AND WEST** ⑮ have plenty of little shops to explore, as does the adjacent **WING LOK STREET** ⑯. Follow Bonham Strand West to **DES VOEUX ROAD WEST** ⑰ to see the dried food and medicine shops. When you're just about ready to turn back, head toward the harbor and follow Connaught Road east until you come to the cream-and-brown **WESTERN MARKET** ⑱, built in 1906. From here it's an easy tram ride back to Central.

TIMING

Allow a full day, perhaps two if you want to spend time shopping for antiques. It's possible to walk from the Star Ferry Terminal to Cat Street in three hours, but you won't be able to see anything in depth. The Man Mo Temple will add 20 minutes. The second half of the walk, from Cat Street to Western Market, will take an hour or two.

Sights to See

❺ **BANK OF CHINA.** When it was built as the bank's headquarters after World War II, this stylish art-deco building was 20 ft higher than the adjacent Hongkong & Shanghai Bank (HSBC). Now one of the smallest buildings in Central, it was utterly dwarfed in the 1980s by a new HSBC building. Not to be outdone, the Bank of China commissioned architect I. M. Pei to build a new headquarters nearby. The resulting **Bank of China Tower**, completed in 1990, was the first building to break the ridgeline of Victoria Peak. It may not be as innovative as the HSBC building, but it dominates Hong Kong's urban landscape. For a panoramic view of Central, head to the 43rd-floor observation deck, open weekdays from 9 to 5 and Saturday 9 to 1. Best of all, it's free. The old building now houses Sin Hua Bank and, on the top floor, David Tang's exclusive China Club, a mix of postmodernism and pre-Communist Shanghai nostalgia. *Garden Rd.*

★ ⓯ **BONHAM STRAND EAST AND WEST.** This thoroughfare is crowded with shops that evoke the old China Coast trade merchants. Bonham Strand West, in particular, is known for its Chinese medicines and herbal remedies. Many of its old shops have their original facades, and inside, the walls are lined with jars of pungent ingredients such as wood bark and insects. Dried and ground up, these are infused in hot water or tea, or taken as powders or pills. A few shops sell live snakes, used in winter soups to ward off colds; snake gallbladders are said to improve virility.

⓱ **DES VOEUX ROAD WEST.** Tram tracks indicate that you've reached the west end of Bonham Strand West. On the left (south) side of the street is a cluster of shops selling preserved foods—from dried and salted fish to black mushrooms to vegetables—and herbal medicines. This is a good area for lunchtime dim sum.

ⓗ **HOLLYWOOD ROAD.** Many of Hong Kong's best antiques, furniture, and classical-art galleries are concentrated at the eastern end of Wyndham Street. As the road heads west, the shops gradually move down-market, selling porcelain, curios, and trinkets masquerading as ancient artifacts. Look to the left for a sign saying POSSESSION STREET, where Captain Charles Elliott of the British Royal Navy stepped ashore in 1841 and claimed Hong Kong for the British empire. It's interesting to note how far today's harbor is from this earlier shoreline—the result of a century of aggressive land reclamation.

★ ⑥ **HONGKONG & SHANGHAI BANK (HSBC).** Designed by Sir Norman Foster as the headquarters of Hong Kong's premier bank, this striking building is a landmark of modern architecture. It sits on props, allowing you to look up through its glass belly into the soaring atrium within. You can also see its inner workings: technical elements—from elevator gears and pulleys to circuit boards—are visible through smoked glass. Completed in 1985 at a time of insecurity vis-à-vis China, at a cost of almost US$1 billion, the building was a powerful statement that the bank had no intention of deserting the Territory. *1 Queen's Rd., Central, across from Statue Sq.*

⑩ **JAMIA MOSQUE.** This attractive gray-and-white mosque was built by HMH Essack Elias of Bombay in 1915, and it shows its Indian heritage in the perforated arches and decorative work on the facade. The mosque itself is not open to non-Muslims, but it occupies a small, verdant enclosure that offers a welcome retreat from the city. It once had a nice view down toward the water, but that was disrupted by an apartment tower—one of many now ringing this site. *30 Shelley St., just off Midlevels Escalator.*

② **JARDINE HOUSE.** To the west of the Star Ferry Terminal, recognizable by its signature round windows, this 1973 building was once the tallest in Central. It houses Jardine, Matheson & Co., the greatest of the old British *hongs* (trading companies) that dominated trade with imperial China. Jardines has come a long way from the days when it trafficked opium, and its investment-banking arm, Jardine Fleming, is one of the most respected in Asia. *Connaught Pl., across from the Central Post Office.*

⑦ **THE LANDMARK.** Few fashion designers, watch craftsmen, or other makers of luxury goods do not have—or do not crave—a boutique in the Landmark. Live concerts are occasionally performed near the fountain in the high-ceiling atrium. *Des Voeux Rd. between Ice House and Pedder Sts. Building, daily 9 AM–midnight; most shops, daily 10–6.*

central and western districts

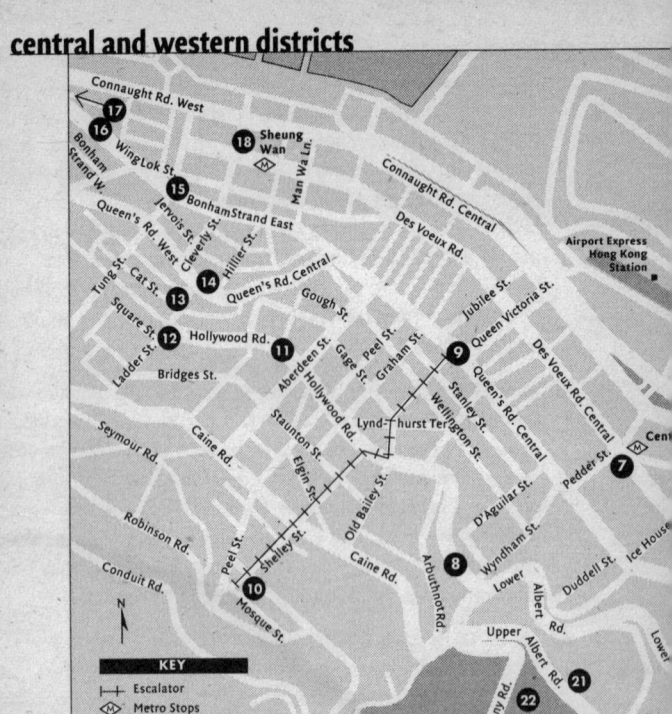

Bank of China, 5
Bonham Strand East and West, 15
Des Voeux Road West, 17
Government House, 21
Hollywood Road, 11
Hongkong & Shanghai Bank, 6
Hong Kong Park, 19
Jamia Mosque, 10
Jardine House, 2
The Landmark, 7
Legislative Council Building, 4
Man Mo Temple, 12
Midlevels Escalator, 9
Peak Tram, 23
Queen's Road Central, 14
St. John's Cathedral, 20
Star Ferry Terminal, 1
Statue Square, 3

17

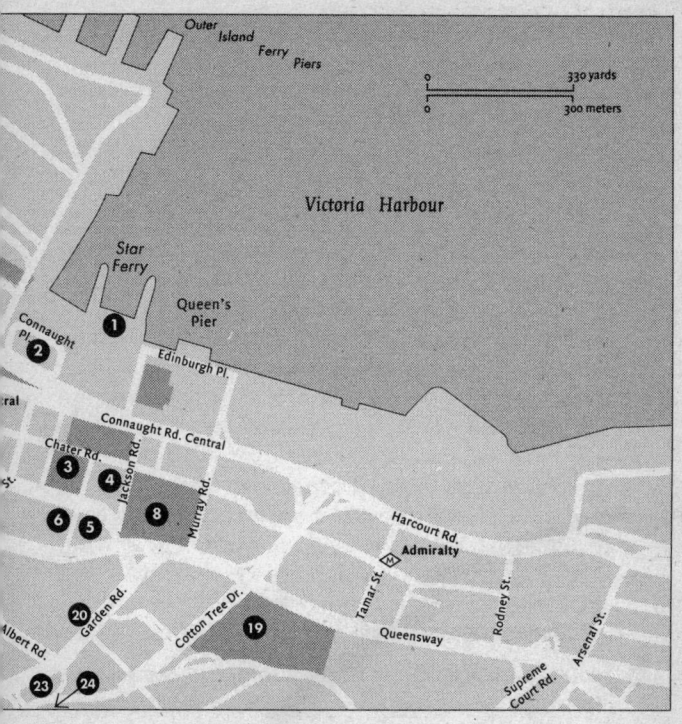

Upper Lascar Row/Cat Street, 13	Wyndham Street, 8
Victoria Peak, 24	Zoological and Botanical Gardens, 22
Western Market, 18	
Wing Lok Street, 16	

④ LEGISLATIVE COUNCIL BUILDING. One of the few grand Victorian structures left in this area, this building was erected for the Supreme Court in 1912 and now home to the Legislative Council (LegCo). The Chinese-style eaved roof is a modest British concession to local culture. In front of the Council Building is the **Cenotaph,** a monument to all who lost their lives in the two world wars. *Statue Sq. at Jackson Rd.*

⑫ MAN MO TEMPLE. Built in 1847 and dedicated to the gods of literature and of war—Man and Mo—this is Hong Kong Island's oldest temple. It is now primarily a smoke-filled haven for elderly women paying respects; enormous spirals of incense hang from the beams. The statue of Man is dressed in green and holds a writing brush, while Mo is dressed in red and holds a sword. To their left is a shrine to Pao Kung, god of justice; to the right is Shing Wong, god of the city. The temple bell, cast in Canton in 1847, and the drum are sounded to attract the gods' attention when a prayer is being offered. To check your fortune, shake one of the bamboo cylinders in front of the altar until a stick falls out. The number on the stick corresponds to a written fortune. The temple will happily sell you the book with the English translation. *Hollywood Rd. at Ladder St. Daily 8–6.*

⑨ MIDLEVELS ESCALATOR. This 1-km-long (½-mi-long) combination of escalators and walkways provides free, glass-covered transport up or down the steep incline between Central and Midlevels. The uphill climb provides a view of the 1915 Jamia Mosque at Shelley Street. **Staunton Street,** one level above Hollywood Road, is now known as Hong Kong's SoHo (South of Hollywood), with an eclectic collection of cafés and bars. From 6 to 10 AM the escalators move downhill, so commuters living in Midlevels can get to work; and after 11:30 they shut down. You can get off at any point and explore the side streets and shops. Almost every building has a tiny makeshift altar to the ancestors, usually made of red paper with gold Chinese characters, with offerings of fruit and incense. *Enter across from Central Market, at Queen's Rd. Central and Jubilee St. Daily 6 AM–11:30 PM.*

⑭ QUEEN'S ROAD CENTRAL. At various points this is one of Hong Kong's most prestigious shopping addresses and among its most traditional streets. Of the countless shops and stalls selling everything imaginable to treat the body's vital energies, the **Eu Yan Sang Medical Hall** (152 Queen's Rd., Central) is the one to visit for an education in traditional Chinese medicines. Glass cases display reindeer antlers, dried fungi, ginseng, and other standard medicinal items; English-language cards explain some of the uses, and men behind the counters will happily sell you purported cures for anything from the common cold to impotence. A note of caution: Chinese medicines are not regulated by the Hong Kong government, and anything that sounds dubious or dangerous might be just that.

★ **❶ STAR FERRY TERMINAL.** Since 1898 the ferry terminal has been the gateway to the island for commuters and travelers coming from Kowloon. First-time visitors are all but required to cross the harbor on the Star Ferry at least once and ride around Hong Kong Island on a double-deck tram. In front of the terminal you will usually see a few red rickshaws; once numbering in the thousands, these two-wheel man-powered taxis are all but gone. *Enter terminal through tunnel next to Mandarin Hotel, Connaught Rd. and Connaught Pl. 1st class HK$2.20, 2nd class HK$1.70. Daily 6 AM–midnight.*

❸ STATUE SQUARE. This piece of land was gifted to the public by the Hongkong & Shanghai Bank, with the proviso that nothing built on it could block the bank's view of the water. The square is named for the statue of Sir Thomas Jackson, Bart. (1841–1915), who was the bank's chief manager for more than 30 years in the late 19th century. The square is surrounded by some of the most important buildings in Hong Kong, including those housing the Hong Kong Club, the Legislative Council, and the Bank of China, and has an entrance to the Central MTR station. On Sunday it becomes the hub for maids enjoying their day off.

- ⓭ **UPPER LASCAR ROW.** Cat Street, as Upper Lascar Row is often called, is a vast flea market. You won't find Ming vases here—or anything else of significant value—but you may come across an old Mao badge or an antique pot or teakettle.

    More worthwhile for the art or antiques collector is the section of shops and stalls known as **Cat Street Galleries** (38 Lok Ku Rd.), adjacent to the flea market, open 10–6 every day but Sunday. This is a new and growing complex, with galleries selling every kind of craft, sometimes old but more often new. You can rest your feet and have coffee in the convenient little European café Somethin' Brewin'.

- ⓲ **WESTERN MARKET.** Erected in 1906, this is the only surviving segment of a larger market building built in 1858. It functioned as a produce market for 83 years. Threatened with demolition, it was exquisitely restored and turned into a unique shopping outlet. Alas, the retail mix is not quite right, with souvenir and trinket shops on the ground floor, fabrics on the middle floor, and a Chinese restaurant on the top floor. But the building, gorgeously decorated with Chinese bunting, is worth a trip. *323 Connaught Rd. W. Daily 10 AM–11:45 PM.*

- ⓰ **WING LOK STREET.** You can find fascinating traditional items on this street lined with shops selling dried fish and seafood, rattan goods, medicines, and the engraved seals called chops. Some shops engrave your initials on a chop made of plastic, bone, or jade. Ivory is also available, but it's illegal to bring it into the United States. It takes about an hour to engrave a chop. *Off Queen's Rd. Central.*

- ★ ⑧ **WYNDHAM STREET.** The galleries that pack the curving block of Wyndham Street from the Fringe Club to where Wyndham becomes Hollywood Road are like miniature museums. Most stores are open daily from 10 to 7, though on Sunday some have shorter hours or are closed. Here you can find Oriental rugs from the Middle East and Central Asia, interesting birdcages, authentic Chinese antiques, Tibetan silk hangings, silverwork, pottery,

Ming and Qing Dynasty reproduction furniture, statues, contemporary Chinese art, and more.

FROM CENTRAL TO THE PEAK

Midlevels is the wide band of land south of Central that runs halfway up Victoria Peak. It has long been one of Hong Kong's most desirable residential districts. Bisecting it is the Midlevels Escalator, which connects Central Market with some of the area's main residential roads. Free of charge and protected from the elements, the escalator moves people through the congested city without destroying the landscape.

Numbers in the margin correspond to numbers on the Central and Western Districts map.

Sights to See

㉑ GOVERNMENT HOUSE. Constructed in 1855, this handsome white Victorian building was the official residence of the British governor. During the Japanese Occupation it was significantly rebuilt, so it now exhibits a subtle Japanese influence, particularly the eaved roof. The SAR's chief executive, Tung Chee Hwa, had no wish to reside here—some say because of perceived negative feng shui—so Government House is used periodically for state occasions. It is not open to the public. *Upper Albert Rd., just west of Garden Rd.*

★ ⓒ **⑲ HONG KONG PARK.** Hoarding 25 acres of prime real estate, this park comprises lakes, gardens, sports areas, a café, a rainforest aviary with 500 species of birds, and a greenhouse with 200 species of tropical and arid-region plants. Some of the artificial rocks and waterfalls in the lower gardens can feel a little unnatural, but the park is a blessedly quiet and lush oasis within the urban melee. The park contains Flagstaff House, the former official residence of the commander of the British forces and the city's oldest colonial building (built in 1846). The house is now the **Museum of Tea Ware,** which chronicles the history of tea and its various accessories from the 7th century on. *Cotton Tree Dr. at park entrance, tel. 2869–0690. Free. Park, daily 6:30 AM–11 PM. Museum, Tues.–Sat. 10–5.*

㉓ PEAK TRAM. Housed in the Lower Peak Tram Terminus is the world's steepest funicular railway. It passes five intermediate stations on its way to the upper terminal, 1,805 ft above sea level. The tram was opened in 1880 to transport people to the top of Victoria Peak, the highest hill overlooking Hong Kong Harbour. Previously, the only way to get to the top was to walk or take a bumpy ride up the steep steps in a sedan chair. The two 72-seat cars are hauled up the hill by cables attached to electric motors. A shuttle bus to and from the Peak Tram leaves from Edinburgh Place, next to City Hall. *Between Garden Rd. and Cotton Tree Dr. tel. 2522–0922. HK$20 one way, HK$30 round-trip. Daily every 10–15 mins 7 AM–midnight.*

⓴ ST. JOHN'S CATHEDRAL. Completed in 1849, this Anglican cathedral was built with Canton bricks in the shape of a cross. It serves as a good example of both Victorian-Gothic and Norman architecture. *4–8 Garden Rd., up from Queen's Rd. Central, on west side of the street just past the large parking lot. Daily 9–5, Sun. services.*

★ **㉔ VICTORIA PEAK.** Known in Chinese as Tai Ping Shan, or Mountain of Great Peace, the Peak is Hong Kong's one truly essential sight. On a clear day, nothing rivals the view of the dense, glittering string of skyscrapers that line Hong Kong's north coast and the carpet of buildings that extend to the eight mountains of Kowloon. It's well worth timing your visit to see the view both by day and at night, perhaps by taking in a meal at one of the restaurants near the upper terminus. The Peak is more than just a view, however; it also contains extensive parkland, perfect for a picnic or a long walk. The **Peak Tower**, the commercial complex of shops, restaurants, and diversions up top, is an attempt to rebrand a visit to the Peak as "the Peak Experience," complete with shopping, amusement parks, and restaurants. This has been a mixed success, but children might enjoy some of the activities.

㉒ ZOOLOGICAL AND BOTANICAL GARDENS. A stroll along quiet pathways lined with semitropical trees, shrubs, and flowers is a delightful way to escape the city's traffic and crowds. In the early morning you can watch people practicing tai chi chuan, the ancient art of meditative shadow boxing. The zoo has jaguars and gorillas, which for years were a source of friction between the government and animal-rights groups, but the cages have been expanded to better simulate the animals' natural habitats. The aviary has more than 300 species of birds, including a spectacular flock of pink flamingos. *Upper Albert Rd., opposite Government House; enter on Garden Rd., tel. 2530–0155. Free. Daily 6:30 AM–7 PM.*

WANCHAI

Originally Wanchai was one of the areas the British set aside for Chinese residences—but it developed a reputation for vice and became a magnet for sailors on shore leave. How times have changed. Wanchai is now quite safe, and at night, it comes alive with bars, restaurants, and discos, as well as establishments offering some of Wanchai's more traditional services.

Numbers in the margin correspond to numbers on the Wanchai, Causeway Bay, Happy Valley, and North Point map.

Sights to See

❷ **ACADEMY FOR PERFORMING ARTS AND HONG KONG ARTS CENTRE.** Hong Kong is often maligned, not least by its foreign residents, as a cultural desert, but these two adjacent buildings have excellent facilities for exhibits and the performing arts. Find out about the busy schedule of activities in local newspapers or at the ticket reservations office. While you're at the Arts Centre, visit the **Pao Gallery** (fourth and fifth floors), which hosts both local and international exhibits. *2 Harbour Rd., Wanchai, tel. 2582–0256. Free. Daily 10–8.*

wanchai, causeway bay, happy valley, and north point

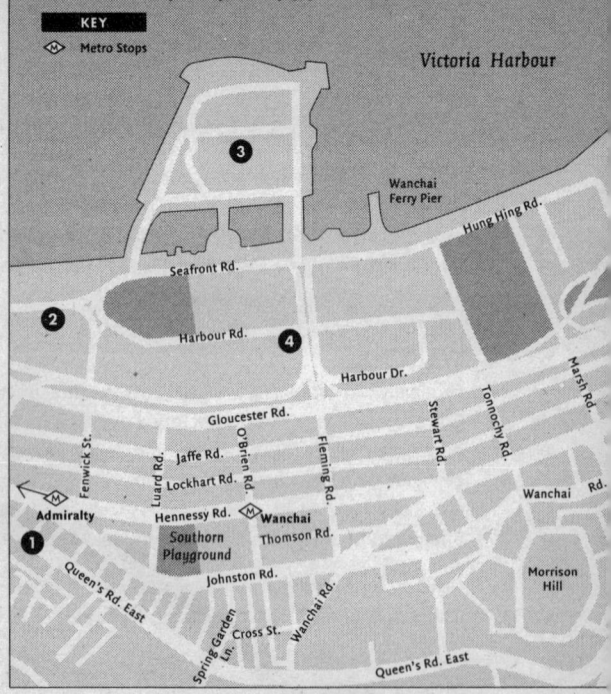

Academy for Performing Arts and Hong Kong Arts Centre, 2	Aw Boon Haw (Tiger Balm) Gardens, 12	Causeway Bay Typhoon Shelter, 8	Happy Valley Racetrack, 13
	Cargo Handling Basin, 6	Central Plaza, 4	Hong Kong Convention and Exhibition Centre, 3

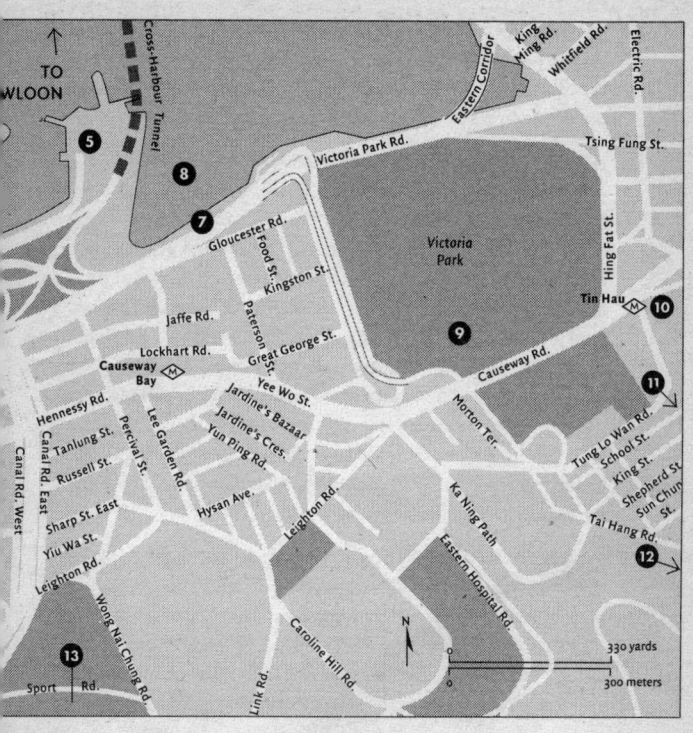

Hong Kong Yacht Club, 5	Queen's Road East, 1
Kwun Yum Temple, 11	Tin Hau Temple, 10
Noonday Gun, 7	Victoria Park, 9

④ CENTRAL PLAZA. In Asia's ongoing race to build ever-taller skyscrapers, this office complex (completed in 1992) briefly held the title as the region's tallest. It has long since been surpassed, but at 78 stories it's still striking. *Harbour Rd. and Fleming Rd.*

③ HONG KONG CONVENTION AND EXHIBITION CENTRE. The original center opened in 1988 as one of the largest and best-equipped meeting facilities in the world, but in typical Hong Kong fashion, it was quickly deemed insufficient. For the 1997 handover ceremonies, the city decided to build, in a mad, furious dash, the extension that now sits prominently on a spit of reclaimed land jutting into the harbor. An exceptionally long walk through the center yields celebratory sculptures commemorating the handover and a waterfront promenade with views of Kowloon. It forms the core of the complex that includes the Convention Plaza office tower, a block of service apartments, and two hotels, the Grand Hyatt and the Renaissance Harbour View. *Enter on Harbour Rd. between Fenwick Rd. and Fleming Rd.*

① QUEEN'S ROAD EAST. Choked with traffic day and night, this busy shopping street is packed with diversions. Rice and food shops and stores sell rattan and traditional furniture, curtains, picture frames, paper lanterns, and Chinese calligraphic materials. Shortly before reaching the Hopewell Centre, is the altar of the **Tai Wong Temple**; you can smell its smoldering joss sticks.

CAUSEWAY BAY, HAPPY VALLEY, AND NORTH POINT

One of Hong Kong's best shopping areas, Causeway Bay also has a wide range of restaurants. Much of the district is easily reached from Central by the tram that runs along Hennessy Road, or by the MTR to the Causeway Bay station. With their offices, apartment blocks, and factories, North Point and Quarry Bay are both undeniable parts of the "real" Hong Kong. From Causeway Bay you can ride the tram for a few miles through these areas.

Numbers in the margin correspond to numbers on the Wanchai, Causeway Bay, Happy Valley, and North Point map.

Sights to See

★ ✋ **⓬ AW BOON HAW (TIGER BALM) GARDENS.** Built in 1935 with profits from sales of a popular menthol balm, the gardens were the pet project of two Chinese brothers, who also built a mansion here. Eight acres of hillside are pocked and covered with grottoes and pavilions filled with garishly painted statues and models of Chinese gods, mythical animals, and scenes from fables and parables. An ornate seven-story pagoda contains Buddhist relics and the ashes of monks and nuns. Be forewarned: some Taoist and Buddhist scenes are decidedly gruesome. *Tai Hang Rd., Happy Valley. Free. Daily 9:30–4.*

❻ CARGO HANDLING BASIN. West of the Yacht Club and east of the Wanchai Ferry pier (which sends ferries to Kowloon), you can watch the unloading of boats bringing cargo ashore from ships anchored in the harbor. *Hung Hing Rd.*

❽ CAUSEWAY BAY TYPHOON SHELTER. This boat basin was originally built as a bad-weather haven for sampan dwellers. In the 1960s and '70s, tourists could have dinner on a sampan, but this is no longer possible, as the number of fishing families who live in those small open-air boats has dwindled and the basin has filled with pleasure craft. A few traditional sampans, crewed primarily by elderly toothless women, still putter around ferrying owners to their sailboats.

⓭ HAPPY VALLEY RACETRACK. Hong Kong gamblers are avid horse-racing fans; the track in Happy Valley opened soon after the British first arrived in the territory. Races are generally held on Wednesday night or weekends from September through June. The joy of the Happy Valley track, even for those who aren't into horses, is that it's smack in the middle of the city and surrounded by towering apartment blocks—indeed, people whose balconies hang over the backstretch often have parties on racing days. Special day-tours allow visitors to experience the exclusive high-roller lounges. However it's just HK$10 to join in at the public stands where feverish gamblers wave their newspapers madly during races. *Hong Kong Jockey Club, 2 Sports Rd., Happy Valley, tel. 2966–8111 or 2966–8364. HK$50 for entrance badge.*

⑤ HONG KONG YACHT CLUB. The yacht club is worth a visit, but it's not open to the public, so you'll need a local who is a member (or knows one) to give you guest privileges. If you belong to a yacht club at home, you may have reciprocal guest privileges. Once inside, you're welcomed by a delightfully old-fashioned bar with magnificent views of the harbor. On weekends the place hums with activity, especially when there are races, common from spring through fall. The South China Sea Race to Manila is held every two years at Easter time; call the race office (tel. 2891–0013) for details. *Kellet Island, off Hung Hing Rd., tel. 2832–2817.*

⑪ KWUN YUM TEMPLE. A shrine to the goddess of mercy has stood on this site for 200 years, but the current structure is mostly new, dating from 1986. Constructed on top of a huge boulder, it has a high ceiling and gallery and is very popular with local worshipers. *Lin Fa Kung St. W. Daily 9–nightfall.*

⑦ NOONDAY GUN. "In Hong Kong they strike a gong and fire off a noonday gun," wrote Noël Coward in his song "Mad Dogs and Englishmen." They still fire that gun at noon each day from a small enclosure overlooking the Yacht Club Basin and Typhoon Shelter, which is reached via a long walk (follow the signs) through the parking garage next to the Excelsior Hotel. The tradition was started by Jardine Matheson and Co., the great hong that inspired James Clavell's novels *Taipan* and *Noble House*. Jardine would fire a salute each time their *taipan*, who ruled over the company like a lord, would enter or leave the harbor. This angered the local governor, who ordered the company to use a gun instead of a cannon, and to fire it only as a noontime signal. The gun itself, with brass work polished bright, is a 3-pound Hotchkiss that dates back to 1901. *Across from Excelsior Hotel, 281 Gloucester Rd.*

❿ TIN HAU TEMPLE. Located on a street of the same name off Causeway Road (behind Park Cinema on the southeast side of Victoria Park), this temple is one of several in Hong Kong similarly named and dedicated to the goddess of the sea. Its decorative roof and old stone walls are worth a peek; the date of construction is unknown, but the temple bell was made in 1747. *Tin Hau St. off Causeway Rd.*

❾ VICTORIA PARK. Beautifully landscaped with trees, shrubs, flowers, and lawns, the park has an aviary and recreational facilities for swimming, lawn bowling, tennis, roller-skating, and even go-cart racing. The Lantern Carnival is held here in mid-autumn, with the trees a mass of colored lights. Just before Chinese New Year (late January–early February), the park hosts a huge flower market. Early every morning the park fills with hundreds of tai chi chuan practitioners. *Gloucester Rd.*

SOUTH SIDE

One of Hong Kong's unexpected pleasures, the South Side consists largely of rolling green hills and a few residential areas around picturesque bays. You can't cover this area on foot, but you can take a city bus or taxi from Central to either Stanley or Shek O (a 20- to 30-minute ride) and walk around.

Sights to See

ABERDEEN. Named after an English lord, not the Scottish city, Aberdeen got its start as a refuge for pirates some 200 years ago. After World War II the *tanka* (boat people) attracted tourists to their floating restaurants. Note the famous Jumbo restaurant just offshore. The tanka still live on houseboats in the harbor, though today their economic conditions are depressing. Much of traditional Aberdeen continues to thrive along side streets, where you can find outdoor barbers at work and any number of dim sum restaurants. In the harbor, some 3,000 junks and sampans are interspersed with floating restaurants. Use a licensed operator for harbor tours, which depart every 20 minutes daily from 8 to 6 from the main Aberdeen seawall opposite Aberdeen Centre. A trip for four to six people should cost from HK$100 to HK$150. Individual tickets are HK$40.

A famous **Tin Hau temple** in Aberdeen, now in a state of decline, has its original bell and drum, which are still used at its opening and closing each day. This is one of several shrines to the goddess of the sea celebrated in the Tin Hau Festival in April and May, when hundreds of boats converge along the shore.

APLEICHAU (DUCK'S TONGUE) ISLAND. Yachts, junks, and sampans are constructed at the boatbuilding yard on this island, and almost all without formal plans. You can travel to the island by sampan, but if you travel by bus, look to your right as you cross the bridge for a superb view of the harbor. Vehicles are not allowed to stop on the bridge, so you'll have to walk if you want to take a picture. On your left is the famous Jumbo Floating Restaurant. Quiet and unspoiled just a decade ago, Apleichau is now bursting at the seams with development.

DEEP WATER BAY. Situated on Island Road, just to the east of Ocean Park, this bay was the setting for the William Holden film *Love Is a Many Splendored Thing* (1955), and its deep coves are still lovely. Nearby are the manicured greens of the exclusive Hong Kong Golf Club. Not surprisingly, the area has become a multimillionaires' enclave and is home to Hong Kong's richest man, Li Ka-shing, a very private real-estate tycoon.

HONG KONG UNIVERSITY. Established in 1911, the university has almost 10,000 undergraduate and graduate students. Most of its buildings are spread along Bonham Road, the most interesting of which is the 19th-century University Hall, designed in a hybrid Tudor Gothic style.

The university's **Fung Ping Shan Museum** has an excellent collection of Chinese antiquities (ceramics and bronzes, some dating from 3000 BC, fine paintings, lacquerware, and carvings in jade, stone, and wood). It also has the world's largest collection of Nestorian crosses from the Yuan Dynasty (1280–1368). The museum is a bit out of the way, but it's a must for the true Chinese art lover. *94 Bonham Rd., tel. 2859–2114. Free. Mon.–Sat. 9:30–6.*

OCEAN PARK AND MIDDLE KINGDOM. One of the world's largest oceanariums, **Ocean Park** (tel. 2873–8888) occupies 170 acres overlooking the sea. On the lowland side are gardens, parks, and a children's zoo. A cable car with spectacular views of the south coast can take you to the headland side and to Ocean Theatre, the world's largest marine-mammal theater. There are also various carnival rides; a new Adventure Bay development is scheduled for completion in 2003. The park is open daily 10–6; adult admission is HK$150. Originally a theme park representing 5,000 years of Chinese history, **Middle Kingdom** (tel. 2873–8583) is undergoing redevelopment. Some say the move is to compete with Disney's $3 billion theme park on Lantau Island due for completion in 2005. The plan aims to create a retail, dining, and entertainment facility. The current dinner-theater production, "The Glory of the Forbidden City," includes Chinese acrobats, Sichuan opera, and *bian lian* or quick face-change acts. *Tai Shue Wan Rd.*

REPULSE BAY. Named after the British warship HMS *Repulse* (not, as some local wags say, after the pollution of its waters), the beach is a wonderful place to while away an afternoon. This was the site of the famed Repulse Bay Hotel, which gained notoriety in December 1941 when invading Japanese clambered over the hills behind it and entered its gardens, which were being used as headquarters by the British. After a brief battle, the British surrendered. The hotel was demolished in 1982 and eventually replaced with a luxury residential building, but replicas of its Repulse Bay Verandah Restaurant and Bamboo Bar were opened in 1986, run by the same people who operated the hotel.

SHEK O. The easternmost village on the south side of Hong Kong Island is a popular weekend retreat. It's filled with old houses, great mansions, a superb golf course and club, a few simple restaurants, a pretty beach, and fine views, albeit marred by some ugly new housing developments. Leave the town square, full of small shops selling inflatable toys and other beach gear, and take the curving path across a footbridge to the "island" of **Tai Tau Chau,** really a large rock with a lookout for scanning the South China Sea. Little more than a century ago, this open water was ruled by pirates. In **Shek O Country Park,** look here for birds that are hard to find in Hong Kong, such as Kentish plovers, reef egrets, and black-headed gulls, as well as the colorful rufus-backed shrike and the ubiquitous, chatty bulbul.

STANLEY. Notorious during World War II as the home of Japan's largest POW camps in Hong Kong, Stanley is now known for its picturesque beaches and its market, where casual clothing and tourist knickknacks are sold at wholesale prices. Hong Kong has dozens of shops offering similar bargains, but it's more fun to shop for them in Stanley's countrified atmosphere. You can also buy ceramics, paintings, and books. The old police station, built in 1859, is open to the public and now houses a restaurant. Past the market, on Stanley Main Street, a strip of restaurants and pubs faces the bay. On the other side of the bay is a Tin Hau temple, wedged between giant new housing estates.

KOWLOON

Just across the harbor from Central, Kowloon Peninsula is an extension of mainland China bounded in the north by the string of mountains that give Kowloon its poetic name: *gau lung*, "nine dragons." The peninsula boasts many of the territory's best hotels as well as a mind-boggling range of shopping options; and no visit to Hong Kong is complete without taking on the commercial chaos of Nathan Road.

The southernmost part of Kowloon is called Tsim Sha Tsui, where a series of cultural buildings lines the waterfront. North of Tsim Sha Tsui are the market districts of Jordan and Mong Kok. Tsim Sha Tsui is best reached by the Star Ferry, while the rest of Kowloon is easily accessible by MTR or taxi.

Numbers in the margin correspond to numbers on the Kowloon Peninsula map.

Sights to See

❸ BIRD GARDEN. The old Bird Market, with its narrow streets of bird shops has been redeveloped to create this attractive outdoor garden. The rumble of each passing train on the nearby tracks sends the birds into a frenzy. The garden is composed of various courtyards filled with trees and surrounded by 70 stalls selling birds, cages, and accoutrements. Plenty of free birds also swoop in to gorge on spilled food and commiserate with their imprisoned brethren. If you make the 10-minute walk from the Prince Edward MTR station, you can enjoy the aromatic approach through a street lined with flower shops. *Yuen Po St. Free. Daily 7 AM–8 PM.*

❷ HONG KONG CULTURAL CENTRE. This stark, architecturally controversial building (which looks best by its flattering nighttime lighting) has tile walls inside and out, sloped roofs, and no windows, though the view of the harbor would be superb. Its concert hall and two theaters host almost every major artist who performs in the territory. Exhibits are occasionally mounted in the atrium, which has its own three-story metallic mural by Van Lau called *The Meeting of Yin and Yang*. In front of the center is a long, two-level promenade with plenty of seating and a view of the entire north coast of Hong Kong. *10 Salisbury Rd., tel. 2734–2010.*

★ ❺ HONG KONG MUSEUM OF ART. The exterior is unimaginative, but inside are five floors of innovatively designed galleries. One is devoted to historic photographs, prints, and artifacts of Hong Kong, Macau, and other parts of the Pearl River delta; other

kowloon

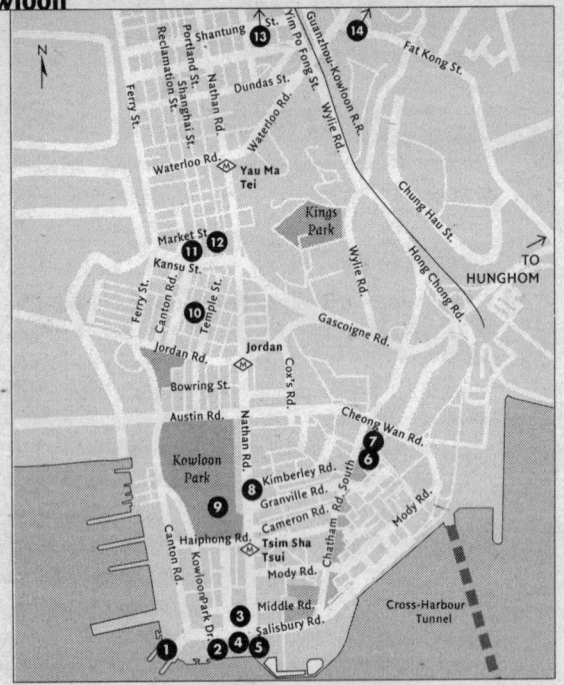

Bird Garden, 13
Hong Kong Cultural Centre, 2
Hong Kong Museum of Art, 5
Hong Kong Museum of History, 7
Hong Kong Science Museum, 6
Hong Kong Space Museum, 4
Kansu Street Jade Market, 11
Kowloon Park, 9
Nathan Road, 8
Peninsula Hotel, 3
Star Ferry Pier, 1
Temple Street, 10
Tin Hau Temple, 12
Wong Tai Sin Temple, 14

galleries feature Chinese antiquities, fine art, and visiting exhibits. *10 Salisbury Rd., tel. 2721–0116. HK$20 for adults, half price Wed. Fri.–Wed. 10–6.*

❼ HONG KONG MUSEUM OF HISTORY. The museum, in an ungainly building adjacent to the Science Museum, covers a broad expanse of Hong Kong's past with life-size dioramas. Exhibits outline 6,000 years of the territory's cultural heritage and history. Special themed exhibits are often on display. *100 Chatham Rd. S, tel. 2724–9042. Free. Tues.–Sat. 10–6, Sun. 1–6.*

★ 🐣 **❻ HONG KONG SCIENCE MUSEUM.** More than 500 scientific and technological exhibits—including an energy machine and a miniature submarine—emphasize interactive participation. The highlight is a series of experiments that test memory and cognitive ability. *2 Science Museum Rd., corner of Cheong Wan Rd. and Chatham Rd., tel. 2732–3232. HK$25 for adults; HK$12.50 concession. Tues.–Fri. 1–9, weekends 10–9.*

🐣 **❹ HONG KONG SPACE MUSEUM.** Across from the Peninsula Hotel, this dome-shape museum houses one of the most advanced planetariums in Asia. Interactive models explain basic aspects of space exploration (though some of these are less than lucid), and fly wires to let you experience weightlessness. At the **Hall of Solar Science,** a solar telescope permits visitors a close look at the sun, and the **Space Theatre** (seven shows daily from 2:30 to 8:30) has Omnimax movies on space travel, sports, and natural wonders. Children under three are not admitted. *10 Salisbury Rd., tel. 2734–2722. HK$10 for exhibits; Omnimax shows: HK$32 front row; HK$24 back row. Mon. and Wed.–Fri. 1–9, weekends 10–9.*

⓫ KANSU STREET JADE MARKET. The old jade market was a sea of pavement trading, but this more orderly market has 450 stalls, selling everything from priceless ornaments to fake pendants. If you don't know much about jade, take along someone who does or you might pay a lot more than you should. Try to come between 10 and noon, as many traders close shop early. *Kansu and Battery Sts. Daily 10–3:30.*

⑨ KOWLOON PARK. The former site of the Whitfield Military Barracks is now a restful, green oasis. The sculpture garden is particularly interesting, and the Chinese Garden has a lotus pond, streams, a lake, and a nearby aviary with a colorful collection of rare birds. The **Jamia Masjid and Islamic Centre,** in the south end of the park near the Haiphong Road entrance, is Hong Kong's principal mosque, albeit not its most graceful. Built in 1984, it has four minarets, decorative arches, and a marble dome. At the northern end of the park sits an extraordinary public swimming complex. *Just off Nathan Rd.*

LEI CHENG UK MUSEUM. This small museum off the beaten path in Sham Shui Po houses a 1,600-year-old vault and is worth a trip for its age alone. The four barrel-vaulted brick chambers form a cross around a domed vault, and the funerary objects are typical of the tombs of the Han Dynasty (AD 25–220). The vault was discovered in 1955 during excavations for the huge housing estate that now surrounds it. To get here, take Bus 2 from Kowloon's Star Ferry terminal to Tonkin Street (drops you closer), or catch the MTR to the Cheung Sha Wan station (faster trip). *41 Tonkin St., Lei Cheng Uk Resettlement Estate. tel. 2386–2863. Free. Mon.–Wed. and Fri.–Sat. 10–1 and 2–6, Sun. 1–6.*

⑧ NATHAN ROAD. The densest shopping street in town, the so-called Golden Mile is actually several miles of hotels, restaurants, and shops of every description. Narrow side streets are lined with even more shops crammed with every possible type of merchandise. Expect to be besieged with street hawkers trying to sell you cheap "Rolexes."

❸ PENINSULA HOTEL. The grande dame of Hong Kong hotels, the Peninsula is a local institution. The exterior is lined with a fleet of Rolls-Royce taxis and doormen in white uniforms, while the huge colonnaded lobby has charm, grandeur, string quartets, and the sedate air of excessive wealth. Even nonguests can stop inside to browse the upscale shopping arcade, partake of high tea, or just marvel at the architecture. *Salisbury Rd., tel. 2366–6251.*

- **① STAR FERRY PIER.** The pier makes a convenient starting point for any tour of Kowloon. Buses depart from the pier to all parts of Kowloon and the New Territories. As you face the bus station, Ocean Terminal, where luxury cruise ships berth, is on your left; inside this terminal, and in adjacent Harbour City, are miles of air-conditioned shopping arcades. To the right of the ferry pier is **Victoria Clock Tower,** which dates from 1915 and is all that remains of the old Kowloon–Canton Railway station. The new station, for travel within China, is 2 km [1 mi] to the east.

- **⑩ TEMPLE STREET.** The heart of a busy shopping area, Temple Street is ideal for wandering and people-watching. By day you'll find market stalls with plenty of kitsch and bargains on clothing, handbags, accessories, and CDs. After 8 PM, the streets become an open-air bazaar of fortune-tellers, prostitutes, street doctors offering cures for almost any complaint, and occasionally Chinese opera. Nearby **Shanghai Street** and **Canton Road** are also worth a peek for their shops and stalls selling everything from herbal remedies to jade and ivory. **Ning Po Street** is known for its paper kites and for the colorful paper and bamboo models of worldly possessions (boats, cars, houses) that are burned at Chinese funerals.

- **⑫ TIN HAU TEMPLE.** One of Kowloon's oldest temples, this sensual site is filled with incense and crowds of worshipers. You'll probably be encouraged to have a try with the fortune sticks, known as *chim* sticks. Each stick is numbered, and you shake them in a cardboard tube until one falls out. A fortune-teller asks you your date of birth and makes predictions from the stick based on numerology. *Market St., 1 block north of Kansu St. Daily 7–5:30.*

★ **⑭ WONG TAI SIN TEMPLE.** Have your fortune told at this large, vivid compound, whose Buddhist shrine is dedicated to a shepherd boy who was said to have magic healing powers. In addition to the main altar, the pavilions, and the arcade—where soothsayers and palm readers are happy to interpret Wong Tai Sin's predictions for a small fee—there are two lovely Chinese gardens and a Confucian Hall. *2 Chuk Yuen Village, Won Tai Sin (in front of MTR stop), tel. 2327–8141. Small donation expected. Daily 7–5.*

In This Chapter

HONG KONG ISLAND 40 • Central and Soho 40 • Admiralty 47 • The Peak 50 • Wanchai 50 • Causeway Bay 53 • Aberdeen 54 • Repulse Bay 54 • Stanley Village 55 • Shek O 56 • KOWLOON 57 • Kowloon City 57 • Sai Kung 57 • Tsim Sha Tsui 59

Updated by Denise Cheung

eating out

WHEREVER YOU GO IN HONG KONG, you're bound to see a restaurant sign. Small living quarters make restaurants the chosen venues for most special occasions and family gatherings. You can find nearly every type of cuisine on earth in Hong Kong.

Don't be shocked when you get your bill: you are charged for everything, including those side dishes placed on every table, which are often mistaken for complimentary snacks. Tips are usually expected (10% average gratuity), even if the bill includes a service charge.

In many Asian restaurants, a table will often order several dishes to share. In this book, the price range given is for an average main dish that is normally shared among two to four diners. Please note that market prices of seafood and prices of outrageously expensive items are not included in the price range to avoid misleading conclusions.

Reservations are always a good idea; we note only when they're essential. We mention dress only when men are required to wear a jacket or a jacket and tie. Unless otherwise noted, the restaurants listed in this chapter are open daily for lunch and dinner.

CATEGORY	COST*
$$$$	over HK$280
$$$	HK$180–HK$280
$$	HK$80–HK$180
$	under HK$80

*per person, not including 10% service charge

HONG KONG ISLAND

CENTRAL AND SOHO

British

$$ ★ **SOHO SOHO.** Traditional dishes are transformed into inspired modern classics at SoHo SoHo. The lamb shank shepherd's pie with parsnip-carrot topping is a success. Don't miss the sticky toffee pudding. The crowds here are a testament to the delicious food and helpful service. *9 Old Bailey St., tel. 2147–2618. AE, DC, MC, V. Closed Sun.*

Chinese

CANTONESE

$$$$ **MAN WAH.** A Zen-like haven in the midst of busy Central, this place serves Cantonese feasts in many courses. The sautéed fillet of sole with chilies in black-bean sauce is nearly a work of art. There's a view of Victoria Harbour. *Mandarin Oriental Hotel, 5 Connaught Rd., tel. 2522–0111 ext. 4025. AE, DC, MC, V.*

$$$ **CHINA LAN KWAI FONG.** Regional Chinese delicacies from Guangdong, Chiu Chow, Szechuan, and Beijing and Shanghai take you on a culinary journey through China. The posh ambience is offset by traditional Chinese touches. Check out the all-you-can-eat dim sum brunch on weekends (HK$128). Reservations are essential for weekday lunch. *17–22 Lan Kwai Fong, tel. 2536–0968. AE, DC, MC, V.*

$$–$$$ ★ **YUNG KEE.** This massive eatery has been in business for more than half a century. The varied clientele—from office workers to visiting celebrities—all receive the same cheerful service. Roast goose is a specialty. Adventurous palates should check out Yung Kee's famous thousand-year-old eggs with ginger. *32–40 Wellington St., tel. 2522–1624. AE, DC, MC, V.*

$ **MAK'S NOODLES LIMITED.** One of the best-known noodle joints in town, Mak's takes pride in its reputation. The premises are clean and the staff is attentive. The menu includes some inventive dishes, but wontons are the real test of a noodle shop, and these are fresh, delicate, and filled with whole shrimp. *77 Wellington St., tel. 2854–3810. No credit cards.*

HUNAN

$$ **HUNAN GARDEN.** Cuisine from the Chinese province of Hunan is famously hot. The fried chicken with chili may well set your lips and throat on fire. There are options for more sensitive palates. Ask for lemon slices with your Shaoxing wine for a zesty aroma. Live Chinese music accompanies your meal. *The Forum, Exchange Sq., 3rd floor, tel. 2868–2880. AE, DC, MC, V.*

SHANGHAINESE

$$$ **SHANGHAI SHANGHAI.** With its art-deco touches, stained glass, and discreet private rooms, this popular restaurant successfully captures the essence of Shanghai in the 1930s. The menu ranges from simple Shanghainese midnight snacks and cold appetizers, to pricey delicacies like abalone. After 9 PM a chanteuse croons Mandarin. Make reservations at least a week in advance. *Ritz-Carlton Hotel, 3 Connaught Rd., basement, tel. 2869–0328. Reservations essential. AE, DC, MC, V. Closed Sun.*

SZECHUAN

$–$$ **SICHUAN GARDEN.** Renowned for its exotic Szechuanese delicacies, this spacious restaurant deserves two thumbs up. Deep-fried bean curd stuffed with mashed shrimp is a must-try item. Good service adds to the overall score. *Gloucester Tower, The Landmark, 3rd floor, tel. 2521–4433. AE, DC, MC, V.*

Continental

$$$$ **MANDARIN GRILL.** A rare find in Hong Kong, this restaurant pairs Colonial atmosphere with impeccable service. Live lobsters and the bouillabaisse are highlights. The Sunday champagne

dining

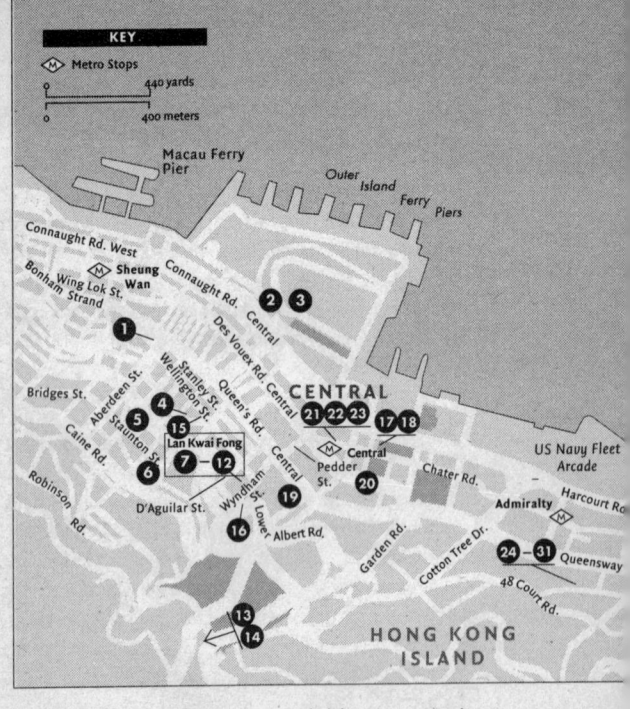

American Peking Restaurant, 32
Blue, 4
The Boathouse, 45
Cafe Deco Bar and Grill, 14
China Lan Kwai Fong, 12
Dan Ryan's, 29
Dim Sum, 48
Dumpling Shop, 37
Eating Plus, 3
El Cid, 54
Fat Angelo's, 40
Forum, 41
Good Luck Thai, 10
Grand Cafe, 38
Grappa's, 30
Grissini, 39
Happy Garden, 46
Hunan Garden, 2
Indochine 1929, 7
Island Seafood & Oyster Bar, 43
Jimmy's Kitchen, 19
Jumbo Floating Restaurant, 47
Lobster Bar, 27
Lucy's, 52
M at the Fringe, 16
Mak's Noodles Limited, 1
Man Wah, 21
Mandarin Grill, 23
Nepal, 5
Nice Fragrance Vegetarian Kitchen, 36

43

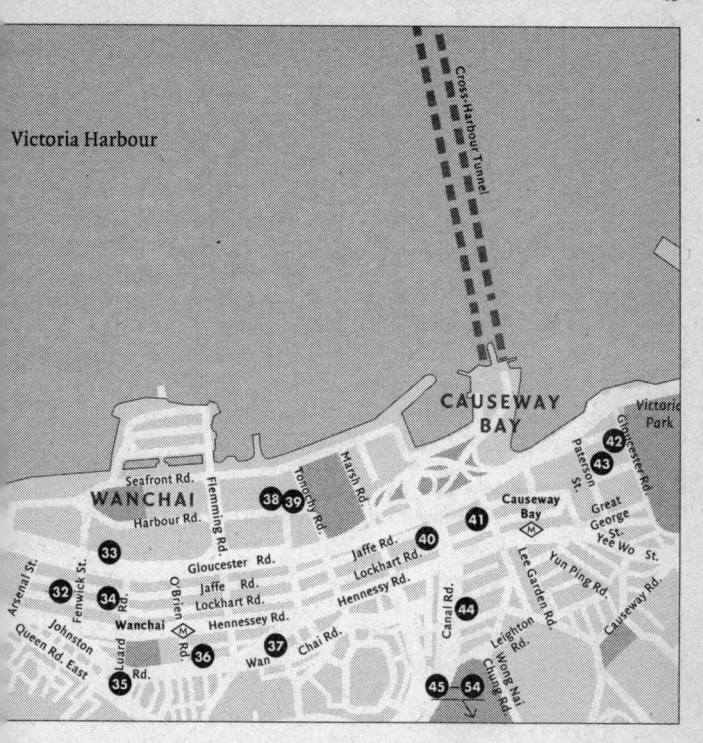

Map of Wanchai and Causeway Bay, Hong Kong, showing Victoria Harbour and the Cross-Harbour Tunnel.

Nicholini's, 25
Open Kitchen, 33
The Pavilion, 15
The Peak Outlook, 13
Petrus, 26
Saigon Beach, 34
Shanghai Shanghai, 17

Shek O Chinese and Thailand Seafood Restaurant, 53
Sichuan Garden, 20
SoHo SoHo, 6
Spices, 50
Stanley's French Restaurant, 51

Steam and Stew Inn, 35
ToTT's Asian Grill & Bar, 42
Thai Basil, 24
Thai Lemongrass, 11
Tokio Joe, 8
Toscana, 18
The Verandah, 54

Vong, 22
W's Entrecote, 44
Ye Shanghai, 28
Yung Kee, 9
Zen, 31

brunch (HK$350) is popular. *Mandarin Oriental Hotel, 1st floor, 5 Connaught Rd., tel. 2522–0111 ext. 4020. Reservations essential. AE, DC, MC, V.*

$$$ **BLUE.** Australian-owned Blue is one of the most stylish restaurants in Hong Kong. High ceilings, soft lighting, and glass-and-chrome furnishings set the scene for fusion dishes. Blue has a good range of pastas and seafood dishes. *43–45 Lyndhurst Terr., tel. 2815–4005. AE, MC, V. No lunch weekends.*

$$$ **M AT THE FRINGE.** ★ Quirky yet classy decor sets this restaurant apart, as does the blend of Continental and Middle Eastern cuisine. The seasonal menu always lives up to expectations, and both vegetarians and carnivores are well served. The set lunch is a good value. *South Block, 2 Lower Albert Rd., 1st floor, tel. 2877–4000. Reservations essential. AE, MC, V. No lunch Sun.*

$$ **THE PAVILION.** A secret gem, the Pavilion resides on a well-hidden alley in the hub of the city. The refined 17th-century French decor is unlike anything else in Hong Kong. Roast cod fillets shares the menu with rack of lamb on rosemary polenta. Sister restaurant **El Pomposo** (*4 Tun Wo La., tel. 2973–0642*), next door, is a mellow spot for a glass of wine and delicious tapas. *3 Tun Wo La., tel. 2869–7768. AE, DC, MC, V.*

Eclectic

$$$$ **VONG.** Designer dining at its height, Vong sits atop the Mandarin Oriental Hotel overlooking Central and the harbor. Celebrated chef-patron Jean-Georges Vongerichten crafts innovative Asian-inspired French dishes. Can't decide? The tasting menu is a sampler of five signature creations. Don't expect a quiet meal: the atmosphere is high-octane. *Mandarin Oriental Hotel, 5 Connaught Rd., 25th floor, tel. 2825–4028. Reservations essential. AE, DC, MC, V.*

$$ **JIMMY'S KITCHEN.** The food is as old-fashioned as the furnishings at this famous 1928 restaurant. Where else in Hong Kong can you

find corned beef and cabbage, borscht, goulash, and bangers and mash? The diverse menu includes Asian delights as well. Rhubarb tart or steamed ginger pudding complete the meal. Reservations are essential for lunch. *South China Bldg., 1 Wyndham St., basement, tel. 2526–5293. AE, DC, MC, V.*

Italian

$$$–$$$$ ★ **TOSCANA.** Classical Italian dining at its finest, Toscana draws visiting regulars from around the world. Huge oil paintings and high ceilings amplify the spacious and elegant interior. Service is friendly, and the food is as opulent as the decor. Pair your meal with little-known wines from Chef Umberto Bombana's list. *Ritz-Carlton, 3 Connaught Rd., tel. 2532–2062. AE, DC, MC, V. Closed Sun.*

Japanese

$$$ **TOKIO JOE.** Funky and casual, this joint has ceramic pots lining faux-fur walls. In the central bar area, you can watch chefs at work, creating classic dishes with a contemporary twist. The house sushi roll is a mixture of deep-fried soft-shell crab, avocado, and crab roe. The courteous staff can recommend a sake that compliments your food. *16 Lan Kwai Fong, tel. 2525–1889. Reservations essential. AE, DC, MC, V. Closed Sun. No lunch.*

Nepali

$$ **NEPAL.** As you eat, take a look at the Nepalese wood carving and the musical instruments and enjoy Indian/Nepalese music in the background. The special Nepalese soup, *golveda-ko-rash*, is an excellent vegetarian dish. The royal chicken is recommended. Equally impressive is Nepal's younger sibling **Kath+Man+Du** (11 Old Bailey St., tel. 2869–1298), serving more modern, and lighter, Nepalese dishes. *14 Staunton St., tel. 2869–6212. Reservations essential. AE, DC, MC, V.*

Thai

$$$ THAI LEMONGRASS. Regional Thai cuisine with a modern twist describes the food at this comfortable spot. Your gourmet tour of Thailand could include sizzling seafood mousse with light red curry and coconut milk. Large windows provide natural light. *30–32 D'Aguilar St., California Tower, 3rd floor, tel. 2905–1688. AE, DC, MC, V. No lunch Sun.*

$ GOOD LUCK THAI. If you're looking for a bargain in the Lan Kwai Fong area, this hole-in-the-wall with alfresco seating is one of your best options. At the dead end of Lan Kwai Fong west, you find hearty and unpretentious Thai food with friendly prices and service. Nearby bars are great choices for a pre-meal aperitif or after-dinner drinks. *13 Wing Wah La., tel. 2877–2971. No credit cards. Closed Sun.*

Vegetarian

$ EATING PLUS. Healthy eating with elegant simplicity is the principle here. Noodles, pastas, and rice dominate the menu. Chicken, beef, and seafood dishes are available. Try the fresh-squeezed juice from the fruit bar. Next to Hong Kong Station, this is a good pre-airport stop. *1009, Southern International Finance Centre, 1st floor, tel. 2868–0599. AE, DC, MC, V.*

Vietnamese

$$$ INDOCHINE 1929. This restaurant resembles a colonial-era French plantation veranda. The food is tasty and authentic; most of the ingredients are imported from Vietnam. Highlights include salt-and-pepper soft-shell crab. This is probably the best Vietnamese food in town. *30–32 D'Aguilar St., California Tower, 2nd floor, Lan Kwai Fong, tel. 2869–7399. AE, DC, MC, V. No lunch Sun.*

ADMIRALTY

American

$$ DAN RYAN'S. ★ This popular bar is often standing-room only. Apart from beer, Dan Ryan's is known for its great burgers—the kind expats dream about when they think of the States. The food is simple, rib-sticking stuff, served without fuss or formality. *114 Pacific Place, 88 Queensway, tel. 2845–4600. Reservations essential. AE, DC, MC, V.*

Chinese

CANTONESE

$$–$$$ ZEN. Upscale and ultrachic, this nouveau-Cantonese eatery has flawless service and dramatic contemporary decor. Deep-fried boneless chicken wings stuffed with glutinous rice have crisp, golden skin. The more standard Cantonese dishes are delicately prepared and presented. *The Mall, Pacific Place One, 88 Queensway, tel. 2845–4555. AE, DC, MC, V.*

SHANGHAINESE

$$$ YE SHANGHAI. The spirit of old Shanghai nightlife is captured at this elegant restaurant ("ye" means "night" in Chinese). Tea-leaf smoked egg appetizers set the stage for entrées like minced chicken with pine nuts and sesame pockets. Reserve early for tables with a view of Queensway. Enjoy live "golden oldies" Thursday through Saturday nights. *Level 3, Pacific Place, 88 Queensway, tel. 2918–9833. AE, DC, MC, V.*

French

$$$$ PETRUS. From the 56th floor of the Island Shangri-La hotel, Petrus looks down on other Hong Kong restaurants in location and culinary standards. Artichoke and truffle terrine melts in your mouth. The extensive wine list is largely French. *Island Shangri-La, Pacific Place, Supreme Court Rd., 56th floor, tel. 2820–8590. Reservations essential. Jacket required. AE, DC, MC, V.*

A Chinese Sampler

The most populous country in the world has dozens of different cooking styles, and five of these are prominent in Hong Kong:

BEIJINGESE. Hearty Beijing cuisine originated in what was once Peking, and was designed for the chilly climate of northern China—noodles, dumplings, and breads are more evident than rice. Peking duck, the perennial favorite, was originally an imperial Mongolian dish. Mongolian or Manchurian hot pots are northern specialties, and firm flavors like garlic, ginger, and leek are popular.

CANTONESE. Because 94% of Hong Kong's population comes from the Chinese province of Guangdong (Canton), Cantonese is by far the most popular culinary style. Favoring meats and fresh vegetables, the Cantonese ideal is to bring out the natural taste of each ingredient by cooking them quickly at very high temperatures. The result is wok chi, a fleeting energy that requires food to be served and eaten immediately.

CHIU CHOW. Originating near Canton, Chiu Chow is a gutsy cuisine that has never caught on in the West. It begins with Iron Buddha tea and moves on to thick shark's-fin soup, whelk (snails), bird's nest, dumplings, and irresistible cold crabs served with vinegar.

SHANGHAINESE. A city of immigrants, Shanghai has cosmopolitan cuisine. And because it lies at the confluence of several rivers, the city has especially good seafood. Rich-flavored Shanghainese hairy crabs are winter favorites. Many Shanghainese dishes are fried in sesame oil or soy sauce and can be greasy. Sautéed freshwater shrimp is a staple. Shanghai is known for its varieties of buns and dumplings.

SZECHUAN. Renowned for spicy flavors, Szechuan food (Sichuan in English) features an eye-watering array of chili types. Szechuan rice, bamboo, wheat, river fish, shellfish, chicken, and pork dishes are prepared with plenty of salt, anise, fennel seed, chili, and coriander. Ingredients are simmered, smoked, and steamed to integrate the flavors—the opposite of Cantonese food.

Italian

$$$$ NICHOLINI'S. Separated by a lounge from Brasserie on the Eighth, this elegant establishment is known for fine Northern Italian fare, with a wide range of pastas, fish, fowl, and meat. Homemade black fettuccine with shrimp, clams, and asparagus tips is deliciously dark. Some wines have been hand-blended for Nicholini's. *Conrad Hotel, Pacific Place, 88 Queensway, 8th floor, tel. 2521–3838 ext. 8210. AE, DC, MC, V.*

$$–$$$ GRAPPA'S. Once inside this restaurant, the mall outside melts away. Nothing on the long list of pastas disappoints. Osso buco smothered in a rich sauce shouldn't be missed. You can stop in simply for superb coffee or one of a range of bottled beers. *132 Pacific Place, 88 Queensway, tel. 2868–0086. AE, DC, MC, V.*

Seafood

$$$ LOBSTER BAR. As the name suggests, lobster is the feature presentation: in soups, appetizers, and entrées. Lobster bisque is creamy and the succulent lobster tartare is served with cucumber salad and two good-size claws. You can also choose from prawns, oysters, scallops, crab cakes, or meat dishes. The space is large and elegant. *Island Shangri-La, lobby level, tel. 2877–3838 ext. 8560. Reservations essential for lunch. AE, DC, MC, V.*

Thai

$$ THAI BASIL. Despite its mall location, this restaurant serves delicious and innovative Asian-contemporary food. The braised lamb shank is highly recommended. Homemade ice-cream flavors range from ginger to honeycomb. The Kitchen, an exclusive area at the back, services well-heeled customers. *Shop 005, Pacific Place, lower ground floor, tel. 2537–4682. AE, DC, MC, V.*

THE PEAK

Eclectic

$$$ CAFE DECO BAR AND GRILL. ★ On a clear day, the views are stunning at this double-decker restaurant overlooking the city. Inside, Chinese, Indian (the kitchen has a proper tandoor), Italian, Mexican, and Thai dishes share the menu. Pizza and pasta choices are always popular. *Peak Galleria, 118 Peak Rd., 1st level, tel. 2849–5111. AE, DC, MC, V.*

$$–$$$ THE PEAK OUTLOOK. The views over Lamma Channel are incredible from the outdoor dining area. When the clouds roll in, the terrace is shrouded in mist, with trees silhouetted in the candlelight. The menu ranges wide from tandoori dishes to barbecue ribs or lobster. The Peak is open for breakfast on weekends. *121 Peak Rd., tel. 2849–1000. AE, DC, MC, V.*

WANCHAI

Chinese

BEIJINGESE

$$ AMERICAN PEKING RESTAURANT. A Hong Kong entity for 40-plus years, this overdecorated restaurant serves favorites like hot-and-sour soup, dumplings, and, in the winter, delicious hot pots. The excellent beggar's chicken must be ordered a day in advance. Authenticity is questionable, but those unaccustomed to Chinese food are well-served. *20 Lockhart Rd., tel. 2527–7770. Reservations essential. AE, DC, MC, V.*

$ DUMPLING SHOP. Even a small portion here is enough for two, so order conservatively. Buns and dumplings, Beijingese specialties, appear in abundance. The staff is friendly and ready to assist. *(576 Nathan Road, tel. 2771–2399). 138 Wanchai Rd., tel. 2836–0000. DC, MC, V (for dinner over HK$200).*

The Dim Sum Experience

Most dim sum restaurants prepare 100 varieties of these traditional tidbits daily and serve them from before dawn to around 5 or 6 PM. Popular dim sum items you need to know include:

CHA SIU BAO: barbecued pork buns

CHA SIU SO: baked barbecued pork pastry

CHEONG FUN: steamed rice rolls (with various fillings such as prawns, beef, barbecued pork, and more)

CHUN KUEN: spring rolls

DAN TART: baked egg tarts

HAR GAU: steamed prawn dumplings with a light translucent wrap

HAR KOK: deep-fried prawn dumplings

LOU MEI GAI: glutinous rice wrapped in lotus leaf

NGAU YUK: steamed beef balls

SIU MAI: steamed pork dumplings

CANTONESE

$ **STEAM AND STEW INN.** Red lanterns lead down an alley to this simple hole-in-the-wall with healthy cooking. Red rice is served and no MSG is used—both rare in Hong Kong. The deep-fried eel is irresistible. There's dim sum at lunchtime. This place draws a young crowd. *21–23 Tai Wong St. E, Wanchai, tel. 2529–3913. MC, V. No lunch Sun.*

Eclectic

$$ **GRAND CAFE.** True to its name, this place is grander than you'd expect. Try the marinated lamb fillet on naan, or you can opt for quesadillas, pastas, Asian-style noodles, free-range chicken, pan-fried veal chops, and oven-glazed king prawns. Desserts are

heavenly. *Grand Hyatt Hotel, 1 Harbour Rd., tel. 2588–1234 ext. 7273. AE, DC, MC, V.*

$ OPEN KITCHEN. Ideal for a pre- or post-performance meal or coffee and pastries, this quiet cafeteria in the Hong Kong Arts Centre has a nice view of Victoria Harbor. Flavors range from Malaysian to British and from Indian to Italian. You can linger or read here undisturbed. *Hong Kong Arts Centre, 2 Harbour Rd., 6th floor, tel. 2827–2923. AE, MC, V (for over HK$150).*

Italian

$$$$ GRISSINI. Catch the aroma of grissini, the Italian breadstick, as you walk through the door. Porcini mushroom and pumpkin risotto is moist and subtly sweet, and roast quail wrapped in pancetta and stuffed with foie gras is rich and flavorful. The 1,000 wines are mainly Italian. *Grand Hyatt, 1 Harbour Rd., 2nd floor, tel. 2588–1234 ext. 7313. Reservations essential. AE, DC, MC, V.*

Vegetarian

$ NICE FRAGRANCE VEGETARIAN KITCHEN. Simple ingredients are whipped into delicious forms here. Try the popular taro paste molded into a fish shape and deep-fried. The succulent "fish" is served with a tangy sweet-and-sour sauce. Vegetarian dim sum rounds out the offerings. *105–107 Thomson Rd., tel. 2838–3608 or 2838–3067. AE, MC, V (over HK$200).*

Vietnamese

$ SAIGON BEACH. Avoid the lunch rush at this tiny spot. The decor is less than impressive, but the authentic Vietnamese fare more than makes up for it. Soft-shell crab and lemon chicken—washed down with French 33 beer—are always a pleasure. Set meals are a good value. *66 Lockhart Rd., tel. 2529–7823. No credit cards.*

CAUSEWAY BAY

Chinese

CANTONESE

$$$$ FORUM. Chef Yeung Koon Yat has earned an international reputation with his Ah Yat abalone, boiled and braised to perfection and served with a rich brown sauce. It is one of the most extravagant dishes in Cantonese cooking. You can also choose from several more affordable Cantonese dishes. *485 Lockhart Rd., tel. 2891–2516. AE, DC, MC, V.*

$$ DIM SUM. This elegant jewel serves dim sum from dusk till dawn.
★ The menu ventures beyond Cantonese, with northern choices like chili prawn dumplings. Lobster bisque and abalone dumplings are popular. There's always a long line for lunch on weekends. Take a tram or a cab to get here. *63 Sing Woo Rd., Happy Valley, tel. 2834–8893. AE, DC, MC, V.*

Contemporary

$$–$$$ TOTT'S ASIAN GRILL & BAR. Talk of the Town sits atop the Excelsior Hotel, overlooking Causeway Bay and the marina. The funky decor—zebra-stripe chairs and a central oval bar—is matched by the East-meets-West cuisine. Red-crab bisque served in a baby papaya is an example. Live music and dancing kicks in late into the evening. *Excelsior Hotel, 281 Gloucester Rd., tel. 2837–6786. AE, DC, MC, V.*

Italian

$$ FAT ANGELO'S. Diners flock here partly for the lively atmosphere and partly for the huge portions of pasta. Dishes serve between four and eight. Favorites are steamed green-lipped mussels in tomato sauce and roast chicken with rosemary. Check out the branches at 49 Elgin Street (tel. 2973–6808) and 29–43 Ashley Road (tel. 2730–4788). *414 Jaffe Rd., tel. 2574–6263. AE, DC, MC, V.*

Seafood

$$–$$$ ISLAND SEAFOOD & OYSTER BAR. In a Causeway Bay shopping area that was once Hong Kong's "Food Street," this laid-back spot is drawing foodies back. Deliciously fresh oysters come in several varieties. Custom-order at the oyster bar: creamy or firm, iced or cooked. The staff gladly makes suggestions. *Shop C, Towning Mansion, 50–56 Paterson St., tel. 2915–7110. AE, DC, MC, V.*

Steak

$$$ W'S ENTRECOTE. At this dining dictatorship you can order steak, steak, or steak. Some call this the best steak in town, and the price includes a salad and as many fries as you can eat. Service is attentive and friendly, and it's a good place for a family meal. *1303 Times Square, 13th floor, tel. 2506–0133. AE, DC, MC, V.*

ABERDEEN

Seafood

$$–$$$ JUMBO FLOATING RESTAURANT. This is it—the floating restaurant you see on postcards. The huge pagoda-shape building burns with a thousand lights at night, and is replete with a throne for visiting emperors. Seafood is the draw: peer into the fish tank and pick your prey. A shuttle ferry to Jumbo departs every two to three minutes from Shum Wan Pier, every 15 minutes from Aberdeen Pier. *Shum Wan Pier Path, Wong Chuk Hang, tel. 2553–9111. AE, DC, MC, V.*

REPULSE BAY

Contemporary

$$$ THE VERANDAH. ★ With palm trees visible through arched teak windows, champagne-cocktail trolleys, and tuxedoed waiters attending your every whim, The Verandah is an unashamed celebration of the halcyon days of colonial rule. A pianist entertains as you sample any of an impressive array of dishes from lobster to lamb. Sunday brunch and afternoon tea are popular. *109 Repulse Bay Rd., tel. 2812–2722. AE, DC, MC, V.*

Pan-Asian

$$ SPICES. Alfresco dining is a rarity in Hong Kong, but at Spices you dine surrounded by lawns and patios. There's also an elegant interior. Main courses include Japanese beef *shogayaki* (panfried fillet with sake sauce). Curry lovers can try varieties from India, Vietnam, Singapore, and Indonesia. *The Repulse Bay, 109 Repulse Bay Rd., tel. 2812–2711. AE, DC, MC, V.*

STANLEY VILLAGE

Contemporary

$$–$$$ THE BOATHOUSE. With a lovely view of the seafront and a cozy decor, this is a perfect spot to hang out with friends and family. A bucket of mussels goes down well with a glass of chilled white wine. Sandwiches and pastas are good bets for casual dining. The wild-berry cobbler sends you home happy. *86–88 Stanley Main St., tel. 2813–4467. DC, MC, V.*

French

$$$ LUCY'S. ★ At this cozy spot, the lighting is low, the decor is warm, and the waiters are friendly and casual. Food is fresh, and dishes lack pretentiousness, but deliver full flavor and satisfaction. Leave room for dessert. *64 Stanley Main St., tel. 2813–9055. MC, V.*

$$–$$$ STANLEY'S FRENCH RESTAURANT. ★ Both floors here have balconies with harbor views, adding to the romantic quasi-Mediterranean atmosphere. The warm lobster salad with artichoke hearts is a favorite. Prix fixe meals are a great bargain. Finish the evening with a selection of cheeses from the Swiss Alps. *90B Stanley Main St., 1st–2nd floors, tel. 2813–8873. Reservations essential. AE, DC, MC, V.*

Spanish

$$–$$$ EL CID. It sounds weird to eat Spanish food at the former British Army Officers' quarters, but this 1848 building is worth a visit. Enjoy tapas and sangria or Rioja as you admire the beautiful sea view. Garlic prawns and stuffed mushrooms are some of the best choices here. Ask for a table with a view. *1st floor, Murray House, Stanley Plaza, tel. 2899–0858. AE, DC, MC, V.*

SHEK O

Pan-Asian

$$ SHEK O CHINESE AND THAILAND SEAFOOD RESTAURANT. Nothing stands out about the food here, but this place is just fun. On summer weekends, people arrive en masse and sit for hours despite the relentless heat. The hybrid cuisine ensures plenty of rice, noodles, and fish. The honey-fried squid is amazing. The festive ambience is a real experience. *303 Shek O Village (main intersection, next to the bus stop), tel. 2809–4426. Reservations essential. AE, DC, MC, V (for over HK$300).*

Thai

$$ HAPPY GARDEN. The name fits—you can tell from the diners' faces. There's nothing fancy here, just simple Thai treats with good prices, huge portions, and swift service. The appetizer sampler is the house specialty. Steamed fish in sour soup is one of the most popular choices. *786 Shek O Village, tel. 2809–4165 or 2809–2770. No credit cards.*

KOWLOON

KOWLOON CITY

Chinese

CANTONESE

$ **TSO CHOI KOON.** Not everyone's cup of tea, Tso Choi (Rough Dishes) corners the market in dishes like fried pig tripe, fried pig brain, double-boiled pig brain . . . you get the idea. The older Hong Kong generation still enjoys this stuff; younger folks may demur. The wary can opt for fried chicken or a fish fillet. *17–19A Nga Tsin Wai Rd., tel. 2383–7170. No credit cards.*

Thai

$–$$ **GOLDEN ORCHID THAI RESTAURANT.** This is some of the best and most innovative Thai cuisine in the territory. The curried crab and the seafood curry in pumpkin are excellent. The steamed seafood cakes, served in Thai stone pots, are also delicious. The Golden Orchid neither levies a service charge nor accepts tips. *12 Lung Kong Rd., tel. 2383–3076. MC, V.*

SAI KUNG

Eclectic

$$ **JASPA'S.** The food here is always deliciously fulfilling, perfect after a day in the countryside. The goat cheese parcel makes a delectable starter, and pasta with bay bugs and lamb chops never disappoint. You can eat on the terrace or inside. *13 Sha Tsui Path, tel. 2792–6388. AE, MC, V.*

Seafood

$–$$ **CHUNG THAI FOOD RESTAURANT AND SEA FOOD.** Chinese and Thai seafood dishes are prepared by chefs of both nationalities.

kowloon dining

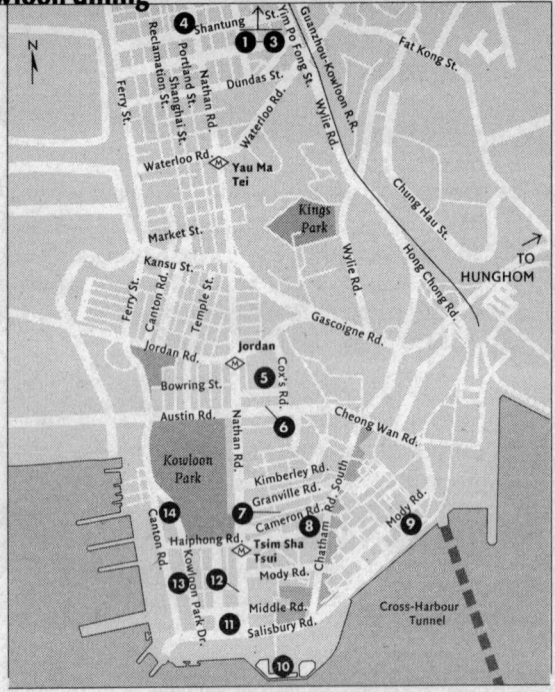

Restaurant	#
The Best Noodle Restaurant	6
Chung Thai Food Restaurant and Sea Food	1
Felix	11
Gaddi's	11
Golden Orchid Thai Restaurant	2
Great Shanghai Restaurant	8
Happy Garden Noodle and Congee Kitchen	14
Jaspa's	4
Kung Tak Lam	7
Lo Chiu Vietnamese Restaurant	5
Mistral	9
Spring Moon	11
T'ang Court	13
Tso Choi Koon	3
Wu Kong	12
Yü	10

Find America
WITH A COMPASS

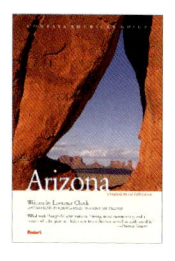

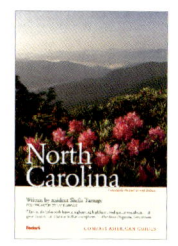

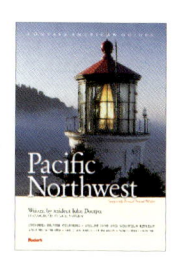

Written by local authors and illustrated throughout with spectacular color images from regional photographers, these companion guides reveal the character and culture of more than 35 of America's most spectacular destinations. Perfect for residents who want to explore their own backyards, and visitors who want an insider's perspective on the history, heritage, and all there is to see and do.

Fodor's COMPASS AMERICAN GUIDES

At bookstores everywhere.

When you pack your MCI Calling Card, it's like packing your loved ones along too.

Your MCI Calling Card is the easy way to stay in touch when you travel. Use it to call to and from over 125 countries. Plus, every time you call, you can earn frequent flier miles. So wherever your travels take you, call home with your MCI Calling Card. It's even easy to get one. Just visit www.mci.com/worldphone.

EASY TO CALL WORLDWIDE

1. Just enter the WorldPhone® access number of the country you're calling from.
2. Enter or give the operator your MCI Calling Card number.
3. Enter or give the number you're calling.

Country	Number	Country	Number
Australia ◆	1-800-881-100	Ireland	1-800-55-1001
China	108-12	Italy ◆	172-1022
France ◆	0-800-99-0019	Japan ◆	00539-121▶
Germany	0800-888-8000	South Africa	0800-99-0011
Hong Kong	800-96-1121	Spain	900-99-0014
		United Kingdom	0800-89-0222

◆ Public phones may require deposit of coin or phone card for dial tone. ▶ Regulation does not permit intra-Japan calls.

EARN FREQUENT FLIER MILES

American Airlines AAdvantage®   CHINA AIRLINES   ▲Delta SkyMiles

K✦REAN AIR   ■UNITED Mileage Plus®   US AIRWAYS DIVIDEND MILES

Limit of one bonus program per customer. All airline program rules and conditions apply.
© 2001 WorldCom, Inc. All Rights Reserved. The names, logos, and taglines identifying MCI products and services are proprietary marks of WorldCom, Inc. or its subsidiaries. All third party marks are the proprietary marks of their respective owners.

MCI

For a bit of spice, try the Thai fried crabs with curry or fried prawns with chili; otherwise, choose any seafood from the store next door, and the chef will prepare it to order. Steaming is highly recommended for fresh fish. *93 Man Nin St., tel. 2792–1481; Seafood shop, 5 Siu Yat Bldg., Hoi Pong Sq., tel. 2792–8172. MC, V.*

TSIM SHA TSUI

Chinese

CANTONESE

$$$–$$$$ **SPRING MOON.** The teak floors, Oriental rugs, and stained glass are all très Shanghai, but the kitchen turns out first-rate Cantonese food. Succulent chicken is marinated in dark soy sauce, and drunken prawns are infused with Shaoxing wine at your table. Tea masters can help you choose from 20 teas. *Peninsula Hotel, Salisbury Rd., tel. 2315–3160. AE, DC, MC, V.*

$$$ **T'ANG COURT.** One of the most elegant Chinese restaurants on the Kowloon peninsula, T'ang Court's modern look is offset by its traditional Chinese cuisine. After covering its bases, the menu gets creative. Lunchtime dim sum are real delicacies. *Great Eagle Hotel, 8 Peking Rd., tel. 2375–1133 ext. 2250. AE, DC, MC, V.*

$ **HAPPY GARDEN NOODLE & CONGEE KITCHEN.** This is the place for down-to-earth Hong Kong fare. A popular breakfast is Cantonese congee and a glutinous rice dumpling wrapped in lotus leaf. Wonton soup or fried rice or noodles makes satisfying lunch. Dinners include diced chicken with cashew nuts and sweet-and-sour pork. *76 Canton Rd., tel. 2377–2603 or 2377–2604. No credit cards.*

SHANGHAINESE

$$ **GREAT SHANGHAI RESTAURANT.** You may not be ready for bold Shanghainese flavors of sea blubber or braised turtle with sugar candy, but do try one of the boneless eel dishes, the beggar's chicken (order before noon for dinner), or the spiced soy duck. The decor is dingy. *26–36 Prat Ave., tel. 2366–8158. AE, DC, MC, V.*

$$ **WU KONG.** You can easily miss the tiny entrance that leads to this first-rate restaurant in a large basement space. Vegetarian goose with vegetables wrapped in crispy bean curd skin is delicious. A whole fish smothered in a piquant sweet and vinegary sauce leaves you wanting more. *Alpha House, 23–33 Nathan Rd., basement (entrance on Peking Rd.), tel. 2366–7244. AE, DC, MC, V.*

$ **THE BEST NOODLE RESTAURANT.** On a side street off Nathan Road near the Jordan MTR station, this humble place is a good choice for a quick bowl of noodles or a simple yet tasty Shanghainese dish. English menus are available. The sweet spareribs are remarkably flavorsome. *105 Austin Rd., tel. 2369–0086 or 2736–2786. No credit cards.*

Contemporary

$$$–$$$$ **FELIX.** ★ On the 28th floor of the Peninsula, Felix's ultramodern space was designed by Philippe Starck. At night, Hong Kong Island glitters from across the harbor through a floor-to-ceiling glass wall. The menu is adventurous—for example, goose liver stuffed with shredded duck meat, onions, and mushrooms served with fresh fig puree. Service is top-notch. *Peninsula Hotel, Salisbury Rd., 28th floor, tel. 2366–6251 or 2315–3188. AE, DC, MC, V.*

French

$$$$ **GADDI'S.** This is one of the few places left where well-trained waiters carry out full service, such as carving a whole braised veal shank at your table. Dishes like poached salmon ravioli with Osetra caviar aim to impress. End with the cheese board or Gaddi's famous soufflé. *Peninsula Hotel, Salisbury Rd., tel. 2315–3171 or 2366–6251 ext. 3989. Reservations essential. Jacket and tie required. AE, DC, MC, V.*

Italian

$$$–$$$$ **MISTRAL.** ★ The clientele here is largely Italian, and the candlelit interior buzzes with conversation. The chef is creative and artistic—

and it's well demonstrated in his cooking and presentation. Pastas are first-rate. You may ask the chef to prepare a special menu according to your taste. *Grand Stanford Inter-Continental Harbour View, 70 Mody Rd., tel. 2731–2870. AE, DC, MC, V. Closed Sun.*

Seafood

$$$$ YÜ. Look elsewhere for food of terrestrial origin. Fresh catches of the day are cooked to suit your tastes. The atmosphere is laid-back, making this a great place to enjoy the unobstructed view of the harbor and, at night, the stunning light show on the island side. *Inter-Continental Hong Kong, 18 Salisbury Rd., tel. 2721–1211. Reservations essential. AE, DC, MC, V. No lunch.*

Vegetarian

$–$$ KUNG TAK LAM. Simple and healthy food—not the no-frills decor—is what makes this place so popular. The cold noodle plates and bean curd ravioli get a big thumbs-up. Set-price meals are incredibly cheap. Its Causeway Bay sibling (Lok Sing Centre, 31 Yee Wo St., tel. 2890–3127) is more elegantly decorated. *45–47 Carnarvon Rd., 1st floor, tel. 2367–7881. AE, DC, V.*

Vietnamese

$–$$ LO CHIU VIETNAMESE RESTAURANT. Look past the spartan interior to the hearty, authentic food. Try not to burn your tongue on the flavorsome lemon grass chicken wings. Deep-fried sugarcane with minced shrimp is sweet and juicy. There's a good variety of noodles and vermicelli served in soup or with fish sauce. *17–19 Hillwood Rd., tel. 2314–7983 or 2314–9211. MC, V.*

In This Chapter

MAJOR SHOPPING AREAS 63 • SHOPPING CENTERS AND MALLS 67 • DEPARTMENT STORES 69 • MARKETS AND BAZAARS 71 • SPECIALTY SHOPPING 72

Updated by Ana Lúcia do Vale

shopping

THE MEGABARGAINS for which Hong Kong was once known have been somewhat diminished. This is not to say you won't find some good values; you just have to know when and where to look.

Beware of absurd discounts (to get you in the door), the switch (after you've paid, they pack a cheaper model), and the heavy, and sometimes physical, push to get you to buy a more expensive item than you want. Know, too, that in spite of the credit-card stickers on the door and in spite of what the card companies say, most stores will insist on cash or add 3%–5% to the total. Shopping at stores with the Hong Kong Tourist Board (HKTB) decal on the window buys you some protection, but if you have trouble, head for the police, the Consumer Council, or the HKTB itself.

ASIAN CAJUN LTD. (12 Scenic Villa Dr., 4th floor, Pokfulam, tel. 2817–3687) leads customized shopping tours for up to four people, for US$100 per hour (not including transportation), with a 3-hour minimum.

MAJOR SHOPPING AREAS

HONG KONG ISLAND

Western District

The Western District is one of the oldest and most typically Chinese areas in Hong Kong. (Take the MTR to Sheung Wan or the tram to Western Market.) The streets behind Western Market are some of the best places to soak up traditional Chinese atmosphere. Wing Lok Street and Bonham Strand West are excellent browsing areas. Visit **She Wong Yuen** (89–93 Bonham Strand) for a taste of snake's-gall-bladder wine. Heading uphill, don't miss the stalls on Ladder Street, which angles down from Queen's Road in Central to Hollywood and Caine roads. Hollywood Road is lined with Chinese antiques and collectibles; it turns into Wyndham Street in Central.

Central District

Many exclusive shops are housed in Central's major office buildings and shopping complexes such as the **Landmark,** on Des Voeux Road, **Prince's Building,** on 10 Chater Road, and **The Galleria at Nine Queen's Road,** all of which are connected by elevated walkways. If couture labels are what you're after, don't miss shopping here among the range of designer boutiques.

In the **Shanghai Tang Department Store** you'll find fine silk Mandarin jackets for men and women, as well as an exciting array of silks and cashmeres in brilliant colors. If you are visiting from Britain, you'll recognize **Marks & Spencer**; however, you may find the discounts here aren't much better than those at home. In the **Jardine House**, at Connaught Place, across from the Central Post Office, check out the **Oxfam Hong Kong** shop in the basement. Even if you are not a secondhand shopper, it's worth a look for all the designer labels selling for a fraction of their original cost.

You can hunt for bargains on clothing, shoes, woolens, handbags, and accessories in the stalls that fill **East and West Li Yuen streets,** between Queen's Road and Des Voeux Road. Watch out for pickpockets. On Wyndham Street you'll find art, antiques, and carpets, and nearby Lan Kwai Fong has art galleries and clothing boutiques in its small office buildings.

Admiralty

Bounded by Central on the west and Wanchai on the east, Admiralty is another mall-crawler's delight. Here you'll find the Admiralty complex that comprises four shopping centers connected by elevated walkways: **Admiralty Centre, Pacific Place, Queensway Plaza,** and **United Centre.**

Wanchai District

The adventurous shopper may find Wanchai interesting. Tattoos are available on Lockhart Road, and traditional Chinese bamboo birdcages on Johnston Road. Dozens of stalls in the lanes between Johnston Road and Queen's Road East sell buttons and bows and inexpensive clothes. Queen's Road East (near the junction with Queensway) is known for shops that make blackwood and rosewood furniture and camphor-wood chests. There are more furniture shops on Wanchai Road, off Queen's Road East.

Causeway Bay

You can get just about anything here. It is dominated by two large Japanese department stores: **Mitsukoshi** and **Sogo**, directly across the street from one another on Hennessy Road. Hennessy Road is filled with smaller shops selling jewelry, watches, stereos, cameras, and electronic goods, and parallel Lockhart Road has several good shoe stores.

The boutiques of Vogue Alley, at the intersection of Paterson and Kingston streets, feature the best of Hong Kong's fashion designers. Just behind the Excelsior hotel is the **In Square (Windsor House),** toward Victoria Park opposite the Park Lane Hotel on Gloucester Road, with a mall plus two floors of computer supplies. The **Chinese Resources Center (CRC)** has a vast selection of goods made in China. **Times Square,** on Matheson Street (on the site of the old Causeway Bay tram station), is a megamall with 12 floors of shopping.

Behind Sogo (away from the waterfront) are Jardine's Bazaar, which has stacks of Chinese restaurants, and Jardine's Crescent, an alley of bargain-basement clothes and accessories. You're not likely to find too many Western sizes. At the end of the alley is a bustling market where Chinese housewives shop for fresh produce and for fresh chickens.

Stanley

Many people visit with the sole purpose of bargain-hunting at Stanley Market. You should allot at least half a day for this market. On the way to Stanley, the shopping arcade at Repulse Bay has several stores selling fine reproductions of traditional Chinese furniture.

KOWLOON

Tsim Sha Tsui District

Locals tend to steer clear of Nathan Road's Golden Mile of shopping, and tourists usually get ripped off there. Stick to the places we list or those displaying HKTB decals. Granville Road, with its embroidery and porcelain shops and clothing factory outlets, is worth a look for serious bargain hunters. Mody Road has souvenir shops.

The **China Products Company** has a fairly wide and good-quality selection of household items. At **Chinese Resources Center** you can buy reasonably priced goods made in China. At **Joyce** you can find chic housewares and clothes by such designers as Issey Miyake and Prada. **Yue Hwa Chinese Products Emporium** has a popular medicine counter.

Harbour City, next to the Star Ferry Pier, is the largest shopping complex in Hong Kong, and one of the largest in the world; if you can't find it here, it probably doesn't exist.

East of Chatham Road, **Tsim Sha Tsui East** is accessible via minibus from the Kowloon Star Ferry. Fifteen shopping plazas are clustered here. Prices are reasonable, but if you are larger than an American size four, you may have trouble finding clothing here.

Hung Hom District

Travel east of Tsim Sha Tsui to Hung Hom, the center of Hong Kong's jewelry and textile industries, for a tremendous selection of bargains in both designer boutiques and factory outlets. Man Yue Street is a good nexus.

Yau Ma Tei and Mong Kok

You could visit this area in conjunction with Nathan Road, but if you're planning a day of hunting and gathering, skip Nathan Road shops and start here. Street signs revert to Chinese, retirees gather to play checkers and mah-jongg in the park, and outdoor markets abound. You can find great deals as well as fakes, pickpockets, and hawking shopkeepers with no-return policies—truly a place to enjoy bargaining and the chaos of it all.

SHOPPING CENTERS AND MALLS

HONG KONG ISLAND

ADMIRALTY COMPLEX comprises four shopping centers, connected by elevated walkways. **Admiralty Centre** has reasonably priced optical shops and men's tailors, a chop maker, and an excellent carpet shop. Perhaps the most popular shopping mall in Hong Kong is glitzy **Pacific Place,** with four floors of upscale shops and restaurants, and its flagship Japanese department store, Seibu. **Queensway Plaza** is dominated by smaller, lesser-name boutiques, which are worth checking out if you want one-of-a-kind buys without having to scour the street markets. The **United Centre** houses several furniture shops. It's worth visiting just for Tequila Kola (☞ Furniture and Furnishings, below), which sells upscale, handcrafted bedroom sets, couches, fabrics, and gifts. *Queensway, Central; MTR: Admiralty.*

CITYPLAZA, one of Hong Kong's busiest shopping centers, is popular with families because of its ice-skating rink, multiplex theater, bowling alley, and weekly cultural shows. Its selection of more than 400 shops includes plenty of clothing options for men, women, and children, and a number of toy stores. *1111 Kings Rd., Taikoo Shing, Quarry Bay. MTR: Taikoo Shing.*

The **LANDMARK** is one of Central's most prestigious shopping sites, housing designer boutiques, art galleries, and fine jewelry shops. A pedestrian bridge links the Landmark with shopping arcades in Jardine House, Prince's Building, the Mandarin Oriental Hotel, and Nine Queen's Road. *Des Voeux Rd. and Pedder St., Central. MTR: Central.*

TIMES SQUARE is a gleaming new complex that packs most of Hong Kong's best-known stores, including Lane Crawford and Marks & Spencer, into 12 frenzied floors. An indoor atrium hosts entertainment ranging from heavy-metal bands to fashion shows; there are also about a dozen eateries, a cinema complex, a popular Japanese supermarket, and two excellent bookstores. *1 Matheson St., Causeway Bay. MTR: Causeway Bay.*

KOWLOON

FESTIVAL WALK is the fanciest mall in Hong Kong. Anchors are the largest Marks & Spencer in town, and a large Esprit. The elite crowds come for Armani Exchange, Calvin Klein, Hong Kong designer Vivienne Tam's boutique, and the Italian handbags at Mandarina Duck. The mall has Hong Kong's largest ice rink. *80 Tat Chee Ave., Kowloon Tong. MTR and KCR: Kowloon Tong.*

HARBOUR CITY is the largest shopping complex in Hong Kong, and one of the largest in the world. It houses Ocean Terminal,

Ocean Centre, Ocean Galleries, and the Hongkong, Marco Polo, and Prince hotels. At last count there were some 50 restaurants and 600 shops. The complex contains a vast Toys "R" Us. *Canton Rd., Tsim Sha Tsui, next to the Star Ferry Terminal. MTR or Star Ferry to Tsim Sha Tsui.*

NEW WORLD SHOPPING CENTRE is a harbor-front shopping center (next to the New World Hotel) with four floors of fashion and leather boutiques, jewelry stores, restaurants, optical shops, tailors, stereo stores, arts and crafts shops, and the Japanese Tokyu department store. *18 Salisbury Rd., Tsim Sha Tsui. MTR: Tsim Sha Tsui.*

DEPARTMENT STORES

CHINESE

CHINA PRODUCTS COMPANY has a fairly wide and good-quality selection of Chinese arts and crafts like pottery, statues, and embroidered materials, as well as everyday household items. *54 Nathan Rd., Tsim Sha Tsui, tel. 2739–3839.*

CHINESE ARTS & CRAFTS is a particularly good bet for fabrics, white porcelain, silk-embroidered clothing, jewelry, and carpets. Our favorite specialty item here is the large globe with lapis oceans and land masses inlaid with semiprecious stones, all for a mere HK$70,000. *Pacific Place, Admiralty; 26 Harbour Rd., Wanchai; Star House, Silvercord Centre; and 233 Nathan Rd., Tsim Sha Tsui; tel. 2827–6667 for information.*

CHINESE RESOURCES CENTER (CRC) has a vast selection of goods made in China, including casual clothing, fancy traditional garb, furniture, teapots, and household appliances ranging from rice cookers to televisions. *488 Hennessy Rd., Causeway Bay, tel. 2577–0222.*

CHUNG KIU CHINESE PRODUCTS EMPORIUM specializes in arts and crafts but also has a good selection of traditional Chinese clothing and fine silk lingerie. *528–532 Nathan Rd., Yau Ma Tei, tel. 2782–1131.*

SHANGHAI TANG DEPARTMENT STORE has an expensive array of silk and cashmere clothing in brilliant colors. Custom-made suits start at around HK$5,000. A custom-made cheongsam (slit-skirt dress with a Mandarin collar) starts at HK$2,500, including fabric. Ready-to-wear Mandarin suits and unisex kimonos are available. There's a second location inside the Peninsula Hotel. *12 Pedder St., Central, tel. 2525–7333.*

YUE HWA CHINESE PRODUCTS EMPORIUM carries a broad selection of Chinese goods such as traditional clothing, statues, tea sets, and embroidered materials. There's also a popular medicine counter. *143–161 Nathan Rd., Tsim Sha Tsui, tel. 2739–3888; 54–64 Nathan Rd., Tsim Sha Tsui, tel. 2368–9165; 301–309 Nathan Rd., Yau Ma Tei, tel. 2384–0084.*

OTHER DEPARTMENT STORES

JOYCE BOUTIQUE has the latest in Western designer fashions for women and men, as well as unique household items. Everything in the hushed interior is beautifully displayed. *New World Tower, 18 Queen's Rd., Central, tel. 2810–1120; Pacific Place, 88 Queensway, Admiralty, tel. 2523–5944.*

LANE CRAWFORD is the most prestigious Western-style department store in Hong Kong, with prices to match. The Central branch is the largest. Special sales here can be crowded. There are branches in Pacific Place, Harbour City, and Times Square. *70 Queen's Rd., Central, tel. 2118–3388.*

MARKS & SPENCER, the famed British retailer, has good-quality clothing in Western sizes as well as a popular specialty food market. Many of the large malls have a branch of this popular store. *28 Queen's Rd., Central, tel. 2921–8321.* •

SEIBU is the most upscale of the Japanese department stores with branches in Hong Kong. In addition to Japanese products, they carry a wide range of Western brands such as Clarks sandals, Timberland boots, and Clinique cosmetics. *Pacific Place, 88 Queen's Way, Admiralty, tel. 2845–4321.*

SINCERE has been around for more than a century. It sells everything from frying pans to jelly beans and has fully stocked makeup counters. Prices tend to be very reasonable. *173 Des Voeux Rd., Central, tel. 2544–2688; 73 Argyle St., Mong Kok, Kowloon, tel. 2394–8233.*

MARKETS AND BAZAARS

THE FLOWER MARKET in Mongkok is a collection of street stalls selling cut flowers and potted plants, with a few outlets specializing in plastic plants and silk flowers. The area takes on an excited hum in the week leading up to the Chinese new year. *Flower St., near Prince Edward MTR station.*

KANSU STREET JADE MARKET displays jade in every form, color, shape, and size. Some trinkets are reasonably priced, but unless you know a lot about jade, don't be tempted to buy something pricey. *Kansu St. off Nathan Rd., Yau Ma Tei. Daily 10–4.*

THE LADIES' MARKET has the same clothing you find in the Temple Street night market, except you can go by daylight. Despite its name, men's and children's clothing are also sold. *Tung Choi St., take Nelson St. exit from the Mongkok MTR station, walk 2 blocks east to Tung Choi St. Daily noon–11.*

STANLEY VILLAGE MARKET's stores open early, at about 10, but close between 5 and 6. **China Town** (39 Stanley Main St.) has well-priced cashmere sweaters, but you get what you pay for as far as quality is concerned. **Sun and Moon Fashion Shop** (18A–B Stanley Main St.) sells casual wear, with bargains on familiar Western brands—some are factory seconds. **Allan Janny Ltd.** (17

Stanley New St.) has antique furniture and porcelain. **Tong's Sheets and Linen Co.** (55–57 Stanley St.) has sheets, tablecloths, brocade pillow covers, and silk kimonos and pajamas. *Bus 6, 6A, or 260 from Central Bus Terminus, Hong Kong Island, or Bus 260 from the Star Ferry; in Kowloon, Bus 973 from Tsim Sha Tsui.*

TEMPLE STREET NIGHT MARKET stretches for almost a mile and is filled with clothes and household items. Cantonese opera performers, pop singers, fortune tellers, and magicians add to the colorful atmosphere. The market is open from 5–10. It's best to hire a local guide to take you; ask at your hotel desk about tours. Some of the surrounding neighborhoods may be unsafe at night. *Kowloon. Near Jordan MTR station.*

SPECIALTY SHOPPING

ANTIQUES
China has laws against taking items more than 120 years old out of the country, but Hong Kong's antiques dealers can, at least officially, sell whatever they want to. Everyday furniture and pottery are not considered national treasures and are not affected by the export laws.

HOLLYWOOD ROAD AND WYNDHAM STREET
At **C. L. Ma Antiques** (43–55 Wyndham St., Central, tel. 2525–4369), find Ming Dynasty–style reproductions, especially large carved chests and tables made of unlacquered wood. **Dynasty Furniture Co.** (68A Hollywood Rd., Central, tel. 2369–6940) has *netsukes* (small statues) skillfully carved out of tagua, a rainforest nut that looks a lot like ivory. Antique and reproduction furniture, screens, and curios can be found at **Eastern Dreams** (47A Hollywood Rd., Central, tel. 2544–2804; 4 Shelley St., Central, tel. 2524–4787).

Honeychurch Antiques (29 Hollywood Rd., Central, tel. 2543–2433) is known especially for antique silver jewelry from

Southeast Asia, China, and England. Along with Japanese, Chinese, and Thai antiques, **Schoeni Fine Arts** (27 Hollywood Rd., Central, tel. 2542–3143) sells Chinese silverware, such as opium boxes, and rare Chinese pottery. **Teresa Coleman** (79 Wyndham St., Central, tel. 2526–2450) carries antique embroidered pieces, including magnificent must-see kimonos. **The Tibetan Gallery** (55 Wyndham St., Central, tel. 2530–4863) sells antique *Thangkas*, or meditation paintings, incense holders, and prayer rugs from Tibet.

True Arts & Curios (89 Hollywood Rd., tel. 2559–1485) has good buys in embroidered items (including minute slippers for bound feet), silver, porcelain, and snuff bottles in its cluttered shop. One of Hollywood's oldest shops, **Yue Po Chai Antique Co.** (132–136 Hollywood Rd., Central, tel. 2540–4374) has a vast and varied stock. Look for traditional wood wedding beds or intricately carved armoires at **Zitan Oriental Antiques** (43–55 Wyndham St., ground floor, Central, tel. 2523–7584), which sells antique furnishings from mainland China.

CAT STREET
The ground-floor cluster of shops, **Cat Street Galleries** (38 Lok Ku Rd., Sheung Wan, Western, tel. 2541–8908), sell porcelain and furniture. Fine furnishings at **China Art** (15 Upper Lascar Row, Western, tel. 2542–0982) are mostly from the Suzhou area of China, and leads tours roughly once a month to its warehouse in southern China.

OTHER AREAS
Altfield Gallery (248–249 Prince's Bldg., 10 Chater Rd., Central, tel. 2537–6370) carries furniture, fabrics, and collectibles from all over Asia. Try **Charlotte Horstmann and Gerald Godfrey** (Ocean Terminal, Tsim Sha Tsui, tel. 2735–7167) for wood carvings, bronzeware, and furniture. **Eileen Kershaw** (Peninsula Hotel, Tsim Sha Tsui, tel. 2366–4083) sells fine Chinese porcelain and jade carvings.

ART

Asian Art News, a bimonthly magazine, sold at bigger newsstands for HK$50, is a good guide to what's happening in galleries around the region. If you want a firsthand look at the latest trends in Asian art, plan to spend a day gallery-hopping in Central and in Lan Kwai Fong.

Alisan Fine Arts Ltd. (Prince's Bldg., Central, tel. 2526–1091) shows a wide range of contemporary art with an East-meets-West flavor. Part of the Fringe Club, **Fringe Gallery** (2 Lower Albert Rd., Central, tel. 2521–7251) is a showcase for young, not-yet-famous Hong Kong artists, both Chinese and expat. **Galeriasia** (1 Lan Kwai Fong, 6th floor, Central, tel. 2529–2598) promotes artists from Asia, with exhibits from Burmese and Vietnamese artists. Work by today's leading Vietnamese artists is showcased at **Galerie La Vong** (1 Lan Kwai Fong, 13th floor, Central, tel. 2869–6863).

Hanart TZ Gallery (Room 202, Henley Bldg., 2nd floor, 5 Queen's Rd., Central, tel. 2526–9019) shows contemporary Chinese artists. Across from the Botanical Gardens, **Plum Blossoms Gallery** (Coda Plaza, 51 Garden Rd., 17th floor, Central, tel. 2521–2189) shows Chinese and Western art, along with antique textiles and Tibetan carpets. The public showroom at **Sandra Walters** (501 Hoseinee House, 69 Wyndham St., Central, tel. 2522–1137) has a wide range of late-19th-century to contemporary Western and Chinese art; call for an appointment. **Schoeni Art Gallery** (U.G. floor, 21–31 Old Bailey St., Central, tel. 2525–5225) exhibits a dramatic mix of abstract, realist, and political paintings by contemporary mainland-Chinese artists.

Wagner Art Gallery (Lusitano Bldg., 4 Duddell St., 7th floor, Central, tel. 2521–7882) is dedicated to introducing Hong Kong to the best Australian artists. **Wattis Fine Art** (20 Hollywood Rd., 2nd floor, Central, tel. 2524–5302) specializes in 18th- to 20th-century European paintings and the work of contemporary local artists. A combination of contemporary Chinese paintings and antique Tibetan silver and carpets is displayed at **Zee Stone Gallery** (Yu Yuet Bldg., 43–55 Wyndham St., Central, tel. 2810–5895). It sells Chinese furniture as well.

AUCTION HOUSES
Watch for auction announcements in the classified section of the *South China Morning Post*.

The prestigious international house **Christie's** (2203 Alexandra House, 22nd floor, 16–20 Chater Rd., Central, tel. 2521–5396, fax 2877–1709) carries very fine and expensive pieces. **Lammert Brothers** (Union Commercial Bldg., 12–16 Lyndhurst Terr., mezzanine floor, Central, tel. 2545–9859) caters to locals with less-expensive goods. The international house, **Sotheby's** (4–4A Des Voeux Rd., Central, tel. 2822–8100, fax 2810–6239), caters to a clientele for whom money is no object. **Victoria Auctioneers** (Century Sq., 1–13 D'Aguilar St., 16th floor, Central, tel. 2524–7611) carries reasonably priced and high-end art and furniture.

CAMERA EQUIPMENT
If in doubt about where to shop for camera equipment, stick to HKTB shops. (Pick up the HKTB shopping guide at any of the board's visitor centers.) All reputable dealers should give you a one-year worldwide guarantee. Always be on the lookout for con jobs. Quite often merchandise is physically switched so that you select one type of camera only to discover later that you've been given a cheaper model. Another ploy is to lure you in with word of a great deal, tell you that particular model is out of stock, and begin an aggressive campaign to sell you a more expensive model. If a shop will not give you a written quote, don't do business with them.

Local photographers shop for equipment at **Photo Scientific Appliances** (6 Stanley St., Central, tel. 2522–1903). Expect good prices on both new and used cameras, lenses, video cameras, and accessories. **Williams Photo Supply** (341 Prince's Bldg., 10 Chater Rd., Central, tel. 2522–8437) stocks an array of photography needs.

CARPETS AND RUGS

China Products Company and Chinese Arts & Crafts provide some of the best selections and price ranges.

Carpet World Ltd. (Shop 271 Ocean Terminal, Harbour City, 3 Canton Rd., Tsim Sha Tsui, tel. 2730–4000) has a wide selection of Chinese carpets. **Chine Gallery** (42A Hollywood Rd., Central, tel. 2543–0023) specializes in Mongolian rugs and carpets. One of the most appealing of the Wyndham shops, **Mir Oriental Carpets** (52 Wyndham St., Central, tel. 2521–5641) has good service and large stock. New selections arrive frequently. The helpful staff at **Oriental Carpet** (41 Wyndham St., Central, tel. 2523–9502) has a large stock of carpets from Iran, Pakistan, Afghanistan, and China. **Oriental Carpets Gallery** (44 Wyndham St., ground floor, Central, tel. 2521–6677) specializes in hand-knotted carpets and rugs from Iran, Afghanistan, Pakistan, and Russia. Highly regarded for its custom-made Chinese rugs, **Tai Ping Carpets Ltd.** (816 Times Sq., 1 Matheson St., Causeway Bay, tel. 2522–7138; Wing On Plaza, 62 Mody Rd., Tsim Sha Tsui East, tel. 2369–4061) allows you to specify color, thickness, and even the direction of the weave. A bit out of the way in a run-of-the-mill shopping mall, **Tribal Rugs Ltd.** (Admiralty Centre, 18 Harcourt Rd., 2nd floor, tel. 2529–0576) sells a variety of rugs from many countries.

CERAMICS

Inexpensive buys can be had in the streets of Tsim Sha Tsui, the shopping centers of Tsim Sha Tsui East and Harbour City, the Kowloon City Market, and the shops along Queen's Road East in Wanchai.

The factory outlet **Ah Chow Factory** (Hong Kong Industrial Centre, 489–491 Castle Peak Rd., Block B, 7th floor, Laichikok, tel. 2745–1511) is a favorite place to score deals. Take the MTR to the Laichikok station; then follow exit signs to Leighton Textile Building/Tung Chau West. **Overjoy Porcelain** (10–18 Chun Pin St., 1st floor, Kwai Chung, New Territories, tel. 2487–0615) is a factory outlet with good bargains. Take the MTR to the Kwai Hing station, then grab a taxi. **Sheung Yu Ceramic Arts** (Vita Tower, 29 Wong Chuk Hang Rd., Aberdeen, tel. 2845–2598) carries good reproductions. Next to Man Mo Temple, **Yue Po Chai Antique Co.** (132–136 Hollywood Rd., ground floor, Central, tel. 2540–4374) is the best place for antique ceramic items.

CHINESE GIFTS

If you're stuck for a gift idea, think Chinese. How about an embroidered silk kimono or a pair of finely painted black-lacquer chopsticks? Or a Chinese chop, engraved with your friend's name in Chinese? For chop ideas, take a walk down Man Wa Lane, in Central near the Wing On department store.

Wonderful *mien laps* (padded silk jackets) are sold in the alleys of Central or in the various shops featuring Chinese products. Another unusual item is a hand-painted Chinese umbrella, available very inexpensively at Chinese Arts & Crafts and China Products Company. Chinese tea, packed in colorful traditional tins, is sold in the teahouses in Bonham Strand and Wing Lok Street in Western. More expensive are padded tea baskets with teapot and teacups, and tiered bamboo food baskets.

CLOTHING

Children

Crocodile Garments Ltd. (Ocean Terminal, Tsim Sha Tsui, tel. 2735–5136) sells Western-style children's clothes. There are other locations all over town. A British firm, **Mothercare** (Windsor House, 311 Gloucester Rd., Causeway Bay, tel. 2882–3468; Prince's Bldg., Central, tel. 2523–5704; Ocean Terminal, Tsim Sha Tsui, tel. 2735–5738) carries baby clothing and maternity wear.

Men's Tailor-Made

Ascot Chang Co. Ltd. (Shop 130, Prince's Bldg., 10 Chater Rd., Central, tel. 2523–3663; Peninsula Hotel, Salisbury Rd., Tsim Sha Tsui, tel. 2366–2398; Regent Hotel Arcade, 18 Salisbury Rd., Tsim Sha Tsui, tel. 2367–8319) has specialized in custom-made shirts for men since 1949. **David's** (Mandarin Oriental Hotel, 5 Connaught Rd., Central, tel. 2524–2979; Wing Lee Bldg., 33 Kimberley Rd., Tsim Sha Tsui, tel. 2367–9556) is an excellent shirtmaker. One of the most famous of all Hong Kong's custom tailors, **Sam's Tailor** (Shop K, Burlington Arcade, 94 Nathan Rd., Tsim Sha Tsui, tel. 2721–8375) has outfitted everyone from European royal families to American and British politicians.

Women's Tailor-Made

Jimmy Chen Co. Ltd. makes suits, dresses, evening dress, outerwear, you name it. At **Linva Tailors** (38 Cochrane St., Central, tel. 2544–2456) one of the best of the old-fashioned cheongsam tailors, prices begin at around HK$2,200 (including fabric and labor) and go up, up, and up. **Mode Elegante** (Peninsula Hotel, Tsim Sha Tsui, tel. 2366–8153) is known for its high-fashion suits for the executive woman. **Sam's Tailor** serves women as impeccably as it serves men. **Shanghai Tang** (12 Pedder St., Central, tel. 2525–7333) makes conservative or contemporary versions of the cheongsam. Men can also have a Chinese *tang* suit made to order.

CLOTHING FACTORY OUTLETS

Discounts on samples and overruns generally run 20%–30% off retail; if you comb through everything, you might bag a fabulous bargain. Check garments carefully for damage and fading: outlets do not accept returns.

Pedder Building

Just a few feet from a Central MTR exit, the **PEDDER BUILDING** (12 Pedder St., Central) contains five floors of small shops. The **Anne Klein Shop** (tel. 2730–8020) is the Pedder Building's only full-fledged retail store. **Blanc de Chine** (tel. 2524–7875) has beautiful Chinese clothes, in styles similar to those at the more famous Shanghai Tang but in subtler colors, plus reproductions of antique snuffboxes as well as silver mirrors and picture frames. **Labels Plus** (tel. 2521–8811) has some men's fashions as well as women's daytime separates. **La Place** (tel. 2868–3163) has youthful fashions, Prada bags, and a large selection of discounted Chanel jackets. **Shopper's World–Safari** (tel. 2523–1950) has more variety than most outlets and a small upstairs department with men's fashions.

Lan Kwai Fong Area

The three streets of this neighborhood are tucked away. Ask a passerby for directions if you have trouble finding it.

The entrance to **Anna's Collection** (Grand Progress Bldg., 15–16 Lan Kwai Fong, 3rd floor, Central, tel. 2501–4955) is under the huge, neon Carlsberg sign. It sells casual clothing, swimwear (up to size 16) and Italian shoes for women that fit American sizes 7 to 11½. Next door to and co-owned by the owner of Anna's Collection, **Evelyn B Fashion** (Grand Progress Bldg., 15–16 Lan Kwai Fong, 3rd floor, Central, tel. 2523–9506) carries business wear, cocktail dresses, and full gowns. **IN Fashion** (9A Grand Progress Bldg., 15–16 Lan Kwai Fong, tel. 2877–9590) carries career wear and casual clothes by Ann Taylor, Laura Ashley, Next, Talbots, and an occasional item designed for Nordstrom, as well as designer ball gowns. **Pot Pourri** (Wong Chung Ming Commercial Bldg., 16 Wyndham St., 12th floor, tel. 2525–1111) sells Talbots, Emanuel Ungaro, and Fenn Wright & Manson. From time to time, **Ricki's** (Cosmos Bldg., 8–11 Lan Kwai Fong, Room 8–11, tel. 2877–1552) carries Emanuel Ungaro, Episode, Donna Karan, Tahari, Jaeger, Ellen Tracy, and Just Cotton. **Zeno Fashions** (Man Cheung Bldg., 15–17 Wyndham St., Block B, tel. 2868–4850) stocks mostly career wear, from labels such as Ellen Tracy, Emmanuel Ungaro, Episode, Krizia, Banana Republic, and Country Road.

Other Outlets

Coast 2 Coast Design Warehouse (Hing Wai Centre, 7 Tin Wan Praya Rd., Room 1904, Aberdeen, tel. 2518–3100) sells clothes, crystal, linens, and ceramics at up to 50% off retail prices. At **Diane Freis Factory Outlet** (Kaiser Estate, Phase I, 41 Man Yue St., Hung Hom, tel. 2362–1760) get discounts of around 30% on Hong Kong–based designer Diane Freis's day-wear concoctions and elaborate cocktail dresses. Ask your hotel concierge about the bus to the outlets in Hung Hom. Many other outlets here have branches in Central, so you may decide it's not worth the trip. Although **Fair Factor** (44 Granville Rd., no phone) has plenty of uninteresting items, you may be rewarded with some real finds—such as items by GAP, Adrienne Vittadini, Villager, and Victoria's Secret for a mere HK$50 to HK$100.

The Joyce Warehouse (34 Horizon Plaza, 2 Lee Wing St., Ap Lei Chau, tel. 2814–8313), in the ritzy Joyce Boutiques in Central and Pacific Place, has taken local shopaholics by storm. Garments by major designers are reduced by about 10% each month, so the longer the piece stays on the rack the less it costs. The outlet is open Tuesday to Saturday 10–6 and Sunday noon–6. Take Bus 90 from Exchange Square and get off at Ap Lei Chau; from there it's easiest to get a taxi to Horizon Plaza, a three- to four-minute ride.

The building may be hard to find, but **Le Baron** (Flat B Yeung Chung, No. 6, Industrial Bldg., 19 Cheung Shun St., 4th floor, tel.

2722–0581) has some of the best cashmere buys in the territory. Get off at Kowloon's Laichikok station. Near the end of Cheung Shun Street, enter through the garage and use the single elevator on the far right. You'll see an office with a sign that says HEYRO DEVELOPMENT CO. LTD. Go into the office, then enter the showroom through the second door on the right. **TSL Jewelry Showroom** (Summit Bldg., 30 Man Yue St., Hung Hom, tel. 2764–4109; Wah Ming Bldg., 34 Wong Chuk Hang Rd., Aberdeen, tel. 2873–2618) has fairly good prices on diamonds and other precious stones in unique settings, and both locations have on-site workshops where you can see the jewelry being made.

COMPUTERS

All the big names sell in Hong Kong. If you plan to buy, make sure the machine will work on the voltage in your country—a PC sold in Hong Kong works on 220 volts, while the identical machine in the United States works on 110 volts. Servicing is another major concern. The real bargains are the locally made versions of the most popular brands. Several malls specialize in computers, peripherals, and electronic equipment, each containing hundreds of shops ranging from small local enterprises to branches of the international brand names. Individual shops usually don't have retail phone numbers.

To buy or repair Apple computers and software, **Lang Tex** (3rd floor, Thomson Commercial Centre, 8 Thomson Rd., Causeway Bay, tel. 2728–0045) is the place to go. Near the Star Ferry Pier in Kowloon, **Star Computer City** (ground floor, Star House, 3 Salisbury Rd., Tsim Sha Tsui) has some good deals on office equipment and desktop computers. **Wanchai Computer Centre** (130 Hennessy Rd., Wanchai) has honest-to-goodness bargains on computer goods and accessories in its labyrinth of shops.

ELECTRONICS

It's important to be certain the TV set or VCR you find in Hong Kong has a system compatible with the one in your country.

Hennessy Road in Causeway Bay has long been the center for stereo gear. Be sure to compare prices before buying, as they can vary widely. Make sure also that guarantees are applicable in your own country. Though most of the export gear sold in Hong Kong has fuses or dual wiring that can be used in any country, it pays to double-check.

The **Fortress** (718–720 Times Sq., 1 Matheson St., Causeway Bay, tel. 2506–0031; Ocean Terminal, Deck 3, Harbour City, Canton Rd., Tsim Sha Tsui, tel. 2735–8628) sells electronics with warranties, a safety precaution that draws the crowds. You can spot Fortress shops by looking for the big orange sign.

FURNITURE AND FURNISHINGS

Hong Kong has seen a tremendous boom in the home-decor market in recent years. Rosewood furniture is a very popular buy in Hong Kong. A number of old-style shops specialize in the rich-looking blackwood furniture that originated in southern China at the turn of the 20th century; look for chairs, chests, couches, and other pieces at the west end of Hollywood Road, near Man Mo Temple. Queen's Road East and nearby Wanchai Road are good sources for camphor-wood chests, as is Canton Road in Kowloon.

Reproductions are common, so "antique" furniture should be inspected carefully. Keep in mind that blackwood, rosewood, and teak must be properly dried, seasoned, and aged to prevent pieces from cracking in climates that are less humid than Hong Kong's. Even in more humid areas, the dryness of winter heating systems can be harmful.

Definitely look on Wyndham Street and Hollywood Road (☞ Antiques, *above*).

The Banyan Tree (Prince's Bldg., Central, tel. 2523–5561; Repulse Bay Shopping Arcade, Repulse Bay, tel. 2592–8721; Ocean Terminal, Harbour City, Tsim Sha Tsui, tel. 2730–6631; Times

Square, 1 Matheson St., Causeway Bay, tel. 2506–3850) has furniture and bric-a-brac, both old and new, from Europe, India, and Southeast Asia. You can arrange to visit Banyan Tree's warehouse by calling its office (tel. 2506–0033). You won't get a discount, but you will have the chance to see—and buy—pieces that have just arrived. **The Banyan Tree Warehouse Outlet** (18/F, Horizon Plaza, 2 Lee Wing St., Ap Lei Chau, tel. 2555–0540) has some discounted items; a Chinese birdcage was recently spotted here for HK$700, an excellent buy. (Lesser-quality birdcages go for more than HK$800 at Stanley Market.)

Cathay Arts (Ocean Centre, tel. 2730–6193) is one of many rosewood-furniture dealers in the Harbour City complex at Tsim Sha Tsui. Furniture outlets at **Horizon Plaza** (2 Lee Wing St., Ap Lei Chau, near Aberdeen) include Shambala, G.O.D. Warehouse, Tequila Kola, Resource Asia, E&H, Antique Express, Inside, Banyan Tree, Dynasty Antiques, and Elmwood.

Queen's Road East, in Wanchai, the great furniture retailing and manufacturing area, offers everything from full rosewood dining sets in Ming style to furniture in French, English, and Chinese styles. Custom-made orders are accepted in most shops here. A cross between IKEA and an Asian boutique, **Tequila Kola** (main showroom: United Centre, Admiralty, tel. 2520–1611) has reproductions of antique wrought-iron beds, one-of-a-kind furniture, home accessories, and jewelry from various corners of Asia.

HANDICRAFTS AND CURIOS
Traditional crafts include lanterns, temple rubbings, screen paintings, paper cuttings, seal engravings, and wooden birds.

The Banyan Tree (☞ Furniture and Furnishings, *above*) carries a pricey but attractive selection of items from several Asian countries. **Kinari** (Anson House, 61 Wyndham St., Central, tel.

2869–6827) sells crafts and antiques from all over Southeast Asia. **Mountain Folkcraft** (12 Wo On La., Central, tel. 2525–3199) has a varied collection of fascinating curios. From Queen's Road Central walk up D'Aguilar Street past Wellington Street, then turn right onto Wo On Lane.

Vincent Sum Designs Ltd. (15 Lyndhurst Terr., Central, tel. 2542–2610) carries Indonesian silver, crafts, and batiks. **The Welfare Handicrafts Shop** (Jardine House, 1 Connaught Pl., Shop 7, basement, Central, tel. 2524–3356; Salisbury Rd., next to the YMCA, Tsim Sha Tsui, tel. 2366–6979) stocks a good collection of inexpensive Chinese handicrafts. All profits go to charity.

JEWELRY

Jewelry is not subject to any local tax or duty, so prices are normally much lower than in most other places. Turnover is fast, competition is fierce, and the selection is fantastic.

Settings of gems will cost less here than in most Western cities, but some countries charge a great deal more for imported set jewelry than for unset gems. Hong Kong law requires all jewelers to indicate on every gold item displayed or proffered for sale both the number of carats and the identity of the shop or manufacturer—make sure these marks are present. Also, check current gold prices, which most stores display, against the price of the gold item you are thinking of buying. For factory outlets, see the HKTB's *Factory Outlets for Locally Made Fashion and Jewellery*.

Chan Che Kee (18 Pottinger St., Central, tel. 2524–1654) has fist-size 14- to 18-karat gold Chinese zodiac animals. Smaller versions can be worn as charms. Other stores on Pottinger Street also carry these animals. **China Handicrafts & Gem House** (25A Mody Rd., Tsim Sha Tsui East, tel. 2366–0973) sells loose gemstones. **Just Gold** (47 Queen's Rd., Central, tel. 2869–

0799; 27 Nathan Rd., Tsim Sha Tsui, tel. 2312–1120) specializes in delicate gold jewelry. Prices exceed HK$5,000. There are branches around town. **Kai-Yin Lo** (The Mall, Pacific Place, Admiralty) has fabulous modern, Asian-influenced jewelry. **The Showroom** (Central Bldg., Pedder St., Room 1203, 12th floor, Central, tel. 2525–7085) specializes in creative pieces using various gems.

Diamonds

For information or advice on buying diamonds in Hong Kong, call the **Diamond Importers Association** (tel. 2523–5497).

Jade

Although jade is Hong Kong's most famous stone, high-quality jade is rare and expensive. Be careful not to pay jade prices for green stones such as aventurine, bowenite, soapstone, serpentine, and Australian jade.

Chow Sang Sang (229 Nathan Rd., Tsim Sha Tsui, tel. 2730–3241) has jade jewelry in traditional Chinese designs. There are smaller branches around town. **Chow Tai Fook** (29 Queens Rd., Central, tel. 2523–7128, and 15 branches) is a good place to shop for fine jade.

Pearls

Freshwater pearls from China, which look like rough grains of rice, are inexpensive and look lovely in several twisted strands.

K. S. Sze & Sons (Mandarin Oriental Hotel, tel. 2524–2803) is known for its fair prices on pearl necklaces and other designs. **Po Kwong** (82 Queen's Rd., Central, tel. 2521–4686) specializes in strung pearls from Australia and the South Seas. **Trio Pearl** (Peninsula Hotel, Tsim Sha Tsui, tel. 2367–9171) has beautiful one-of-a-kind designs in pearl jewelry.

LEATHER BAGS AND BELTS

Italian bags, belts, and briefcases are popular in Hong Kong, but you'll pay top dollar for them. Locally made items are clearly of inferior quality. For bargains, check out designer knockoffs on Li Yuen streets East and West and in Central. Medium-quality bags and belts from local manufacturer Goldlion are sold at Chinese Arts & Crafts. For top-name international products, visit department stores and the Japanese stores in Causeway Bay, Mitsukoshi, and Sogo.

LINENS, SILKS, EMBROIDERIES

Pure silk shantung, silk velvet, and printed silk crepe de chine are just some of the exquisite materials available in Hong Kong at reasonable prices. China Products Company, Chinese Arts & Crafts, and Yue Hwa Chinese Products Emporium have the best selections. Ready-to-wear silk garments are good buys at Chinese Arts & Crafts.

Irish linen, Swiss cotton, Thai silk, and Indian, Malay, and Indonesian fabric are among the imported cloths available. Vincent Sum Designs specializes in Indonesian batik; there's also a small selection at **Mountain Folkcraft** (☞ Handicrafts and Curios, *above*).

The best buys from China are hand-embroidered and -appliquéd linen and cotton. A magnificent range of tablecloths, napkins, and handkerchiefs can be found at **China Products Company** and **Chinese Arts & Crafts** and in linen shops in Stanley Market. Try, too, the various shops on Wyndham and On Lan streets in Central. Beware of machine-made embroidered items being passed off as handmade.

MARTIAL ARTS SUPPLIES

There are hundreds of martial-arts schools and supply shops in Hong Kong, especially in the areas of Mong Kok, Yau Ma Tei, and Wanchai, but they're often hidden away in backstreets and up narrow stairways. The most convenient place to buy your drum cymbal, leather boots, whip, double dagger, studded wrist bracelet, and other kung-fu exotica is **Kung Fu Supplies Co.** (188 Johnston Rd., Wanchai, tel. 2891–1912).

SHOES

The best place to buy shoes in Hong Kong is on Wong Nai Chung Road, in Happy Valley, next to the racetrack. It's hard to find a women's size 8 or larger. In department stores and shopping centers, prices for designer shoes will be similar to those back home.

Kow Hoo Shoe Company (Prince's Bldg., 1st floor, Central, tel. 2523–0489) has great cowboy boots in knee-high calfskin. Renowned for skillful copies of specific styles, **Luen Fat Shoe Makers** (19–21B Hankow Rd., Tsim Sha Tsui, tel. 2376–1180) custom-makes reasonably priced shoes for men and women. **Mayer Shoes** (Mandarin Oriental Hotel, Central, tel. 2524–3317) has an excellent range of styles and leathers for men and women.

TEA

Cha (Chinese tea) falls into three categories: green (unfermented), black (fermented), and oolong (semifermented). Tea sold in attractive tins make inexpensive and unusual gifts. Walk down Queen's Road West and Des Voeux Road West and you'll see dozens of tea merchants and dealers. You can also buy packages or small tins of Chinese tea in large supermarkets.

Long-standing **Cheng Leung Wing** (526 Queen's Rd. W, no phone) is in the heart of the tea district. Dreamland for the sophisticated tea shopper, **Fook Ming Tong Tea Shop** (Prince's Bldg., Central, tel. 2521–0337) has superb teas in beautifully designed tins and antique clay tea ware. Other branches are at the Mitsukoshi and Sogo stores in Causeway Bay, Ocean

Streetwise Shopping

No matter why you come to Hong Kong, it's highly unlikely that you'll leave without having bought something. Hong Kong does a roaring trade in bargain-priced luggage because so many travelers run out of space in their suitcases.

Here are some tips for getting the best deals and avoiding the tourist traps:

- Don't confine yourself to the main roads if you're bargain-hunting. Space is at a premium, and shops appear in unexpected places.
- If you're just browsing, make this very clear; don't be pushed into a purchase.
- Always ask for discounts—especially when making multiple purchases. Expect 10% to 50% off; more at outdoor markets. Only Japanese department stores and some of the larger boutiques fail to discount.
- Don't be shy. Bargain. This is the accepted and expected way of conducting business all over Asia.
- Don't take the salesman's word for it when he assures that his price is the "very best." Shop around.
- Once you've decided on an item, go to the shop of choice first thing the following morning. Remind the salesperson that you are the first customer; it's a superstition that works in your favor. Local shopkeepers believe if they sell to the first customer who walks into their store, they will have a good business day.
- Dress down at outdoor markets. Being well dressed will not help your bargaining position.
- Inspect the goods you buy very carefully; many are seconds.
- When you buy clothing, inspect the item handed to you to avoid taking home a different, seriously flawed item.
- Credit cards and traveler's checks are widely accepted, but surcharges are common; cash is usually best.
- Get a fully itemized receipt for any major purchase.

Terminal, Harbour Centre, and Tsim Sha Tsui. **Tea Zen** (House for Tea Connoisseurs, 290 Queen's Rd., ground floor, Central, Sheung Wan, tel. 2544–1375) offers a range of teas in a simple atmosphere.

WATCHES

When buying a watch, remember Hong Kong's talent for imitation. Stick to officially appointed dealers carrying the manufacturers' signs if you want to be sure you're getting the real thing. When buying an expensive watch, check the serial number against the manufacturer's guarantee certificate and ask the salesperson to open the case to check the movement serial number. If the watch has an expensive band, find out whether it comes from the original manufacturer or is locally made, as this will dramatically affect the price (originals are much more expensive). Always obtain a detailed receipt, the manufacturer's guarantee, and a worldwide warranty.

City Chain Co. Ltd. (Times Sq., 1 Matheson St., Shop 609–610, Causeway Bay, tel. 2506–4217), with locations all over Hong Kong, has a wide selection of watches for various budgets.

In This Chapter

NIGHTLIFE 91 • Bars 91 • Cocktail and Piano Bars 92 •
Nightclubs and Discos 93 • Hostess Clubs 94 • Pubs 94 • Wine
Bars 95 • THE ARTS 96 • Performing Arts Centers 96 • Chinese
Opera 97 • Dance 97 • Film 98 • Music 98 • Theater 99

Updated by Eva Chui

nightlife and the arts

NIGHTLIFE

HECTIC WORKDAYS make way for an even busier night scene in Hong Kong. Though this city is surprisingly safe, the art of the tourist rip-off has been perfected. Check out cover and hostess charges before you get too comfortable, and pay with cash for each round of drinks as it's served. You can pick up a free listing of approved restaurants and nightspots at any Hong Kong Tourist Board (HKTB) information office.

You must be over 18 to buy alcohol. Drugs and unlicensed gambling are illegal. The police are generally helpful, but they expect everyone to know the meaning of *caveat emptor* (buyer beware). Many clubs have a "members only" policy, but usually this just means that visitors must pay a cover charge.

BARS

Cozy **Barco** (42 Staunton St., Central, tel. 2858–1487) has a small lounge area and a courtyard in the back. After a hectic day, **Brown** (18 Sing Woo Rd., Happy Valley, tel. 2891–8558; 30 Robinson Rd., Midlevels, tel. 2971–0012) is a great place to sink into a sofa and chill. High ceilings give it an airy atmosphere. Writers, artists, and travelers gravitate toward **Club 64** (12–14 Wing Wah La., Lan Kwai Fong, Central, tel. 2523–2801), where you can get a reasonably priced drink in a humble setting.

Sophisticated guys and dolls flock to **Alibi** (73 Wyndham St., Central, tel. 2167–1676), a cool bar that's wall to wall with bodies most nights. There's fine dining upstairs. Cosmopolitan and trendy, **Le Jardin** (10 Wing Wah La., Lan Kwai Fong, Central, tel. 2526–2717) has a lovely outdoor terrace. The **Mandarin Oriental** (5 Connaught Rd., Central, tel. 2522–0111) is home to the Chinnery Bar and Captain's Bar, where the smart, Cohiba-cigar set meets to discuss the day's business or to enjoy a post-meeting drink. **Tango Martini** (3/F, Empire Land Commercial Centre, 81–85 Lockhart Rd., Wanchai, tel. 2528–0855) has a stylish and sophisticated lounge and an adjoining restaurant.

Singles mix happily at ultramodern **California** (32–34 D'Aguilar St., Lan Kwai Fong, Central, tel. 2521–1345), one of the hottest places to be seen. California has a late-night disco most nights. **Club Cubana** (47B Elgin St., Central, tel. 2869–1218) stays open late and has a smallish dance floor and small courtyard in back. Hip favorite **Drop** (basement, On Lok Mansion, 39–43 Hollywood Rd., entrance off Cochrine St., Central, tel. 2543–8856) may take some effort to find, but it has the best DJ in town on weekends. Drop claims to be members only, but a little confidence and a lot of dazzle go a long way.

The **Fringe Club** (2 Lower Albert Rd., Lan Kwai Fong, Central, tel. 2521–7251) is the headquarters for Hong Kong's alternative arts scene, and normally stages live music twice a week. **Phibi** (basement, 79 Wyndham St., entrance off Pottinger St., Central, tel. 2869–4469) is a laid-back bar that plays dance music. It gets going around 11 PM. Affectionately known by locals as the Vodka Bar, the **V 13** (13 Old Baily St., SoHo, tel. 8208–1313) teems with locals and expats who enjoy hearty libations.

COCKTAIL AND PIANO BARS

If you'd like a window seat at any of these establishments, request one when making a reservation. The Regent's **Club Shanghai** is decorated in 1930s Chinese style. You won't be out of place if you don your tight-fitting *cheongsam* dress here. Before 9:30 the band performs love songs; later you can hear jazzier tunes. High-altitude harbor gazing is the main attraction at the Island Shangri-La's 56th-floor music lounge **Cyrano** (2 Pacific Place, Supreme Court Rd., 88 Queensway, Hong Kong, tel. 2820–8591), which draws a young crowd.

Felix (Salisbury Rd., Tsim Sha Tsui, tel. 2366–6251), at the Peninsula Hotel, has a brilliant view of the island, and the impressive bar and disco were designed by Philippe Starck. Check out the padded disco room. **Gripp's** (Harbour City, Tsim Sha Tsui, tel. 2113–0088), in the Marco Polo Hong Kong hotel, draws the executive set with nightly entertainment and spectacular harbor views. At the Excelsior's **Talk of the Town** (281 Gloucester Rd., Causeway Bay, tel. 2837–6786), or ToTT's, you're treated to a 270° vista of Hong Kong Harbour.

NIGHTCLUBS AND DISCOS

Entrance to the smarter houses of dance can be HK$100 or more, though this usually entitles you to two drinks.

Glitzy nightspot **Club 97** (9–11 Lan Kwai Fong, Central, tel. 2810–9333 or 2186–1819) draws mobs of beautiful people, and its members-only policy is selectively enforced. If any foreign celebrities are in town, this is where they'll be partying. The club is open from 9 PM to 4 AM. The nightly entrance fee is about HK$97. Unchallenged in its party-hard reputation, **Joe Bananas** (23 Luard Rd., Wanchai, tel. 2529–1811) strictly excludes the military and people dressed too casually. Lines form after 11 PM.

JJ's (Grand Hyatt, 1 Harbour Rd., Hong Kong, tel. 2588–1234) is revered for its flashy disco lights and resident band. Wall-to-wall businessmen and their escorts lounge here. One of the most popular gay clubs in the territory, **Propaganda** (1 Hollywood Rd., lower ground floor, Central, tel. 2868–1316) has a stylish bar area and a dance floor. Go-go boys flaunt their wares at the lap poles. Crowds arrive well after midnight; the entrance fee is HK$70 to HK$160, depending on the time and day.

Practically a disco institution, **Rick's Cafe** (53–59 Kimberly Rd., Luna Court, Tsim Sha Tsui, tel. 2311–2255) remains popular despite its age. If you arrive after midnight on a weekend, be prepared to stand in line. In the basement of the Park Lane Hotel, **Stix** (310 Gloucester Rd., Causeway Bay, tel. 2839–3397) has a large dance floor that fills up with groovers enjoying the house band's pop covers.

HOSTESS CLUBS

Hong Kong's better establishments are multimillion-dollar operations with hundreds of hostess-companions, large dance floors, live bands, dozens of luxurious private rooms with the ubiquitous karaoke setup. The best clubs are on a par with music lounges in deluxe hotels, though they cost more. Peak hours are 10 PM–4 AM. Many hostess-oriented clubs are prostitution fronts.

Club BBoss (tel. 2369–2883), in Tsim Sha Tsui East's Mandarin Plaza, is the grandest and most boisterous hostess club. This is tycoon territory—a bottle of brandy can cost HK$18,000. Along the harbor, in New World Centre, is **Club Deluxe** (tel. 2721–0277), a large, luxurious dance lounge. **Mandarin Palace** (24 Marsh Rd., tel. 2575–6551) is a grand yet comfortable Wanchai nightclub where clients can indulge their singing aspirations in karaoke duets with hostesses until the wee hours.

PUBS

British-managed **Bull & Bear** (10 Harcourt Rd., Hutchison House, Central, tel. 2525–7436) attracts all types, serves standard pub fare, and can get rowdy on weekends. The pioneer of Hong Kong Irish pubs, **Delaney's** (basement, 71–77 Peking Rd., Tsim Sha Tsui, tel. 2301–3980; 2/F, 1 Capital Place, 18 Luard Rd., Wanchai, tel. 2804–2880) has Guinness on tap and a menu of Irish specialties. Happy hour runs from 3 to 8 PM. **Dublin Jack** (37 Cochrine St., Central, tel. 2543–0081) serves Guinness and Irish ales and airs the latest football games.

Western crowds gather at the wood-paneled **Mad Dogs** (basement, Century Sq., 1 D'Aguilar St., Central, tel. 2810–1000), in the Lan Kwai Fong area. If it's not too hot, relax at an outdoor table at Causeway Bay's **King's Arms** (Sunning Plaza, 1 Sunning Rd., tel. 2895–6557), a great place to meet fellow travelers. In Tsim Sha Tsui, a diverse, crowd frequents Aussie-style **Kangaroo Pub** (35 Haiphong Rd., tel. 2376–0083), which has good pub food and views of Kowloon Park. **Ned Kelly's Last Stand** (11A Ashley Rd., Tsim Sha Tsui, tel. 2376–0562) is an institution, with Aussie-style beer tucker (pub grub), and rollicking live jazz in the evening.

The **Old China Hand Hand** (104 Lockhart Rd., tel. 2893–5980) has been here since time immemorial. The decor suffers accordingly, but the pub atmosphere is intact. Sober up with greasy grub after a long night out. Local hangout **Rick's Cafe** (53–59 Kimberly Rd., Luna Court, Tsim Sha Tsui, tel. 2311–2255) is a restaurant–pub à la *Casablanca*, with potted palms, ceiling fans, and posters of Bogie and Bergman.On Knutsford Terrace, a trendy out-of-the-way strip in Tsim Sha Tsui, Caribbean-inspired **Bahama Mama's** (4–5 Knutsford Terr., tel. 2368–2121) has tropical rhythms and kitsch props. With its genuine English antiques, you wouldn't think that **Chasers** (2–3 Knutsford Terr., tel. 2367–9487) would be as groovy as it is, but live pop music draws a regular crowd.

WINE BARS
Tiny, classy **Juliette's** (6 Hoi Ping Rd., Causeway Bay, tel. 2882–5460) provides a cozy ambience for chuppie (Hong Kong's Chinese yuppies) couples and corporate types. For an intimate encounter, try **Le Tire Bouchon** (45A Graham St., Central, tel. 2523–5459), where fine wines accompany tasty bistro meals. Hip, bistro-style **Staunton's Wine Bar & Cafe** (10–12 Staunton St., Central, tel. 2973–6611) is partly alfresco. It's a Sunday-morning brunch favorite.

THE ARTS

A free weekly newspaper, HK Magazine, is distributed each Friday to many restaurants, stores, and bars. The South China Morning Post has an entertainment pullout every Friday called 24/7. The other English-language newspaper, iMail, has a weekend guide on Friday called iMag. **URBTIX** (tel. 2734–9009) outlets are the easiest places to buy tickets for most performances; there's one at City Hall and one at the Hong Kong Arts Centre. The free monthly newspaper City News lists City Hall events.

PERFORMING ARTS CENTERS

Hong Kong Island

City Hall (5 Edinburgh Pl., by Star Ferry, Hong Kong Island, tel. 2921–2840) presents classical music, theatrical performances, films, and art exhibitions. You can buy tickets for cultural events held in government centers from booths on the ground floor by the main entrance. The **Hong Kong Academy for Performing Arts** (1 Gloucester Rd., Wanchai, tel. 2584–8500) has two major theaters, plus a 200-seat studio theater and a 500-seat outdoor theater for music, dance, and drama. The **Hong Kong Arts Centre** (2 Harbour Rd., Wanchai, tel. 2582–0232) has auditoriums, rehearsal halls, and recital rooms. Innovative entertainment and art exhibits take place at the **Hong Kong Fringe Club** (2 Lower Albert Rd., Central, tel. 2521–7251). Shows range from jazz to avant-garde drama, and from the blatantly amateur to the dazzlingly professional. **Queen Elizabeth Stadium** (18 Oi Kwan Rd., Wanchai, tel. 2591–1346) is basically a sports arena, but the 3,500-seat venue presents ballets and music concerts as well.

Kowloon

The 12,000-plus-seat **Hong Kong Coliseum** (9 Cheong Wan Rd., Hung Hom railway station, Hung Hom, tel. 2355–7234) presents everything from basketball to ballet, and from skating polar bears to pop stars. The **Hong Kong Cultural Centre** (10 Salisbury Rd., tel. 2734–2009) facility contains the Grand Theatre, seating 1,750, and a concert hall seating 2,100. The center is used for operas, ballets, and orchestral concerts. The modern **University Hall** (224 Waterloo Rd., tel. 2339–5182) often hosts pop concerts. The space usually caters to local talent.

CHINESE OPERA

Contact the Urban Council (tel. 2922–8008) for performance schedules and details.

There are 10 **Cantonese Opera** troupes in Hong Kong, as well as amateur "street opera" groups that perform in the Temple Street Night Market, at temple fairs, or at City Hall. The art form is highly complex—every gesture has a meaning, and there are 50 gestures for the hand alone. Props attached to the costumes are similarly intricate and are used in exceptional ways. It's best to have a local acquaintance translate the gestures, since the stories are very complicated. The highly stylized **Peking Opera** employs higher-pitched voices than Cantonese opera. It is also older, and more respected for its classical traditions. Well-regarded visiting troupes from the People's Republic of China perform at City Hall or at special temple ceremonies.

DANCE

The **City Contemporary Dance Company** (tel. 2326–8597) presents innovative programs with Hong Kong themes at indoor and outdoor venues. The Western-oriented **Hong Kong Ballet** (tel. 2573–7398) is Hong Kongs first ballet company and vocational ballet school. Since 1981, the **Hong Kong Dance Company** (tel. 2853–2642) has been promoting the art of Chinese dance and choreographing new works with historical themes. The 30-odd members are experts in folk and classical dance.

FILM

Hong Kong reigns as the capital of Asian martial-arts movies. Other movies are mostly B-grade. For show times and theaters, check the listings in HK magazine, the *South China Morning Post*, and the *iMail*.

For art-house features, visit **Broadway Cinematheque** (Prosperous Garden, 3 Public Square St., Yau Ma Tei, tel. 2388–3188; 2384–6281 to reserve tickets). The **Cine-Art House** (ground floor, Sun Hung Kai Centre, Wanchai, tel. 2827–4778) is a quaint two-theater complex that shows films from Japan and the West. **The Hong Kong Arts Centre** (2 Harbour Rd., Wanchai, tel. 2582–0232) screens some of the best independent, classic, documentary, and short films from around the world.

MUSIC

Classical

The **Hong Kong Chinese Orchestra** (tel. 2853–2622) performs only Chinese works. The **Hong Kong Philharmonic Orchestra** (tel. 2721–2030) comprises almost 100 musicians from Hong Kong, the United States, Australia, and Europe. It performs everything from classical to avant-garde to contemporary music by Chinese composers.

Jazz and Folk

The aptly named **Jazz Club** (2/F, California Entertainment Bldg., 34–36 D'Aguilar St., Central, tel. 2845–8477) offers a wide selection of excellent local jazz, R&B, and soul acts as well as top-notch international acts every month. **Ned Kelly's Last Stand** is a haven for pub meals and Dixieland, courtesy of Ken Bennett's Kowloon Honkers. Get here before 10 PM for a good seat. **The Wanch** (54 Jaffe Rd., tel. 2861–1621) features live local folk and rock performances. The Hong Kong–theme decor is worth a visit.

THEATER

The **Chung Ying Theatre Company** (tel. 2521–6628) stages plays—most written by local playwrights—mainly in Cantonese. The group also organizes exchanges with overseas theater companies; venues vary. The **Fringe Club** (2 Lower Albert Rd., Central, tel. 2521–7251) hosts alternative professional and amateur shows. Contemporary plays by American and English writers are sometimes presented. **Zuni Icosahedron** (tel. 2893–8419), the best-known avant-garde group in Hong Kong, stages multimedia drama and dance, usually in Cantonese, at various locations.

In This Chapter

HONG KONG ISLAND 102 • Central 102 • Admiralty 103 •
Midlevels 106 • Wanchai 106 • Causeway Bay 108 • Happy
Valley 109 • North Point 109 • Quarry Bay 110 • KOWLOON 110 •
Hung Hom 110 • Tsim Sha Tsui 112 • Tsim Sha Tsui East 117 •
Yau Ma Tei and Mong Kok 118

Updated by Tobias Parker

where to stay

IT NO LONGER MATTERS whether you stay "Hong Kong side" or "Kowloon side," thanks to the three tunnels that run underneath the harbor, the Star Ferry, and the Mass Transit Railway (MTR, or subway). The new airport rail link whisks you over the Tsing Ma Suspension Bridge through Kowloon to Central in about 25 minutes.

Accommodations can be expensive, but almost no one pays the quoted rate. Travel agents in Hong Kong and abroad frequently offer huge discounts or package deals. Hotels do their part, too, offering discounts and credits for their restaurants and bars. Book your room well in advance for a trip to Hong Kong, especially in March and from September through early December, the high seasons for conventions and conferences.

For an overview of Hong Kong meeting, convention, and incentive facilities, contact the **Convention and Incentive Department** (Hong Kong Tourist Bureau, 10/F, Citicorp Centre, 18 Whitfield Rd., North Point, Hong Kong Island, tel. 2807–6543). The **Hong Kong Tourism Board** (HKTB, www.discoverhongkong.com) publishes the *Hotel Guide*, which lists rates, services, and facilities for all of its members.

We always list the facilities available, but we don't specify whether they cost extra; so when pricing accommodations, always ask what's included and what's not. Hong Kong hotels operate on the European Plan, i.e., with no meals included. Rooms have private baths unless otherwise noted.

CATEGORY	COST*
$$$$	over HK$2,500
$$$	HK$1,800–HK$2,500
$$	HK$1,100–HK$1,800
$	under HK$1,100

*All prices are for a standard double room, excluding 10% service charge and 3% tax.

HONG KONG ISLAND

CENTRAL

$$$$ ★ **MANDARIN ORIENTAL.** Long acclaimed as one of the world's great hotels, the elegant Mandarin Oriental has served the well-heeled and the business elite since 1963. Efficient service and a highly professional staff set it apart. The rooms are designed for luxury rather than mere efficiency, and have antique maps and prints, traditional wood furnishings, and glamorous black-and-gold accents. World-renowned Vong is on the top floor. 5 Connaught Rd., tel. 2522–0111, fax 2810–6190, www.mandarin-oriental.com/hongkong. 502 rooms, 40 suites. 4 restaurants, 3 bars, in-room data ports, in-room safes, minibars, room service, indoor pool, barbershop, hair salon, health club, dry cleaning, laundry service, concierge, business services. AE, DC, MC, V.

$$$$ ★ **RITZ-CARLTON.** An air of refinement is coupled with superb hospitality at this rare gem of a hotel. European antiques and reproductions mix with Asian accents. Rooms are elegant yet comfortable, and overlook either Victoria Harbour or Chater Garden. The attention to detail is nonpareil. The main restaurant, Toscana, serves northern Italian cuisine. The business center has computer workstations with Internet access and color printers. 3 Connaught Rd., tel. 2877–6666; 800/241–3333 in the U.S., fax 2877–6778, www.ritzcarlton.com. 187 rooms, 29 suites. 5 restaurants, bar, lounge, in-room data ports, in-room safes, minibars, 13 no-smoking floors, room service, pool, health club, shop, dry cleaning, laundry service, concierge, business services. AE, DC, MC, V.

ADMIRALTY

$$$$ CONRAD INTERNATIONAL. Spacious rooms at this luxurious business hotel look down from the top 21 floors of a 61-story oval tower rising from Pacific Place, giving dramatic views of the harbor and city. Executive rooms have in-room Internet access, fax machines, and personal step machines. The Brasserie has French fare and views of the park; Nicholini's is one of the city's top Italian restaurants. *Pacific Place, 88 Queensway, tel. 2521–3838, fax 2521–3888, www.conrad.com.hk. 467 rooms, 46 suites. 4 restaurants, bar, in-room data ports, in-room safes, minibars, room service, pool, health club, dry cleaning, laundry service, concierge, business services. AE, DC, MC, V.*

$$$$ ISLAND SHANGRI-LA. ★ Nearly 800 sparkling Austrian crystal chandeliers greet you as you walk through the door. The world's largest Chinese landscape painting, *The Great Motherland of China* hangs from the 39th through the 55th floors in the glass-topped atrium. The staff prides itself on Asian hospitality. Suites have DVD players. Dine well at the renowned French eatery Petrus, the classy Lobster Bar, and the imperial Summer Palace. The health club and outdoor pool overlook Hong Kong Park. *Supreme Court Rd., 2 Pacific Place, 88 Queensway, tel. 2877–3838; 800/942–5050 in the U.S., fax 2521–8742, www.shangri-la.com. 531 rooms, 34 suites. 4 restaurants, bar, in-room data ports, in-room safes, minibars, 4 no-smoking floors, room service, pool, barbershop, hair salon, health club, dry cleaning, laundry service, concierge, business services. AE, DC, MC, V.*

$$$$ J. W. MARRIOTT. This elegant American-style hotel caters to business travelers. Its glass-wall atrium lobby has a cascading waterfall and is filled with plants. Modern rooms have harbor and mountain views and ample work space. JW's California Grill serves California cuisine, and the Cigar Bar has a walk-in humidor with more than 100 types of stogies. The 24-hour gym is well-equipped. *Pacific Place, 88 Queensway, tel. 2810–8366; 800/228–9290 in the U.S., fax 2845–0737, www.marriotthotels.com. 602 rooms, 25 suites.*

lodging

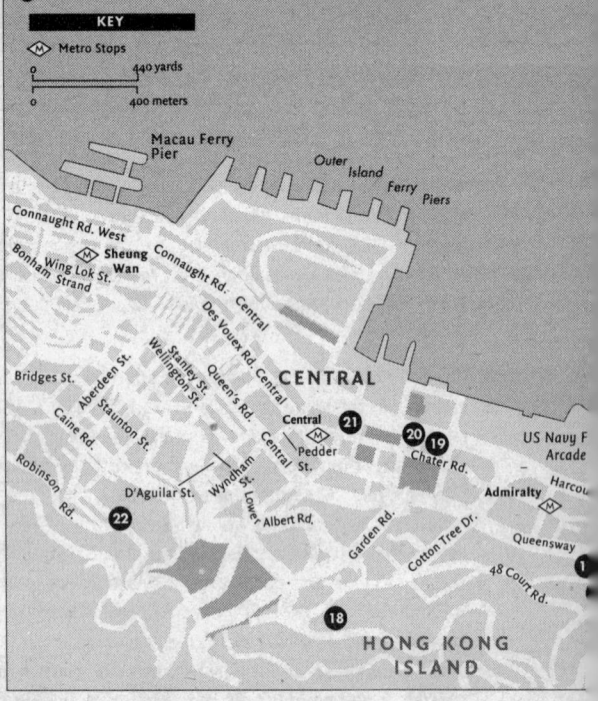

KEY
- Metro Stops
- 0 — 440 yards
- 0 — 400 meters

Bishop Lei International House, **22**
Century, **9**
Century Inn North Point, **1**
Conrad International, **16**
Emperor Happy Valley, **8**
The Excelsior, **4**
Furama, **19**
Garden View International House, **18**
Grand Hyatt, **11**
Grand Plaza, **7**
Harbour View International House, **13**
Island Shangri-La, **17**
J.W. Marriott, **15**
Luk Kwok, **12**
Mandarin Oriental, **21**
New Cathay, **6**

Newton, 2

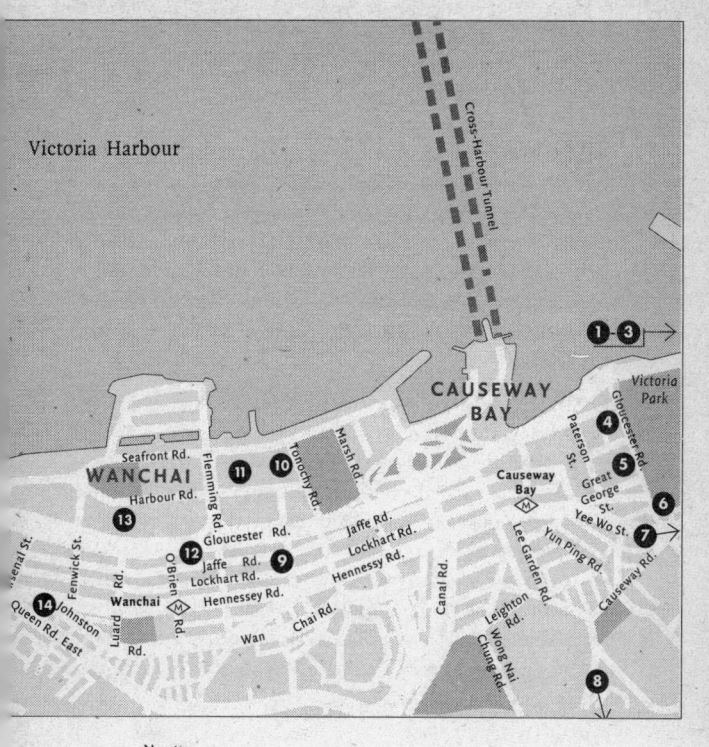

Park Lane, 5

Regal Hongkong Hotel, 3

Renaissance Harbour View, 10

Ritz-Carlton, 20

The Wesley, 14

4 restaurants, 3 bars, in-room data ports, in-room safes, minibars, 14 no-smoking floors, room service, pool, health club, dry cleaning, laundry service, concierge, business services. AE, DC, MC, V.

MIDLEVELS

$$ BISHOP LEI INTERNATIONAL HOUSE. The Catholic diocese operates this guest house in a residential area. Rooms are clean and half have harbor views. The restaurant serves Chinese and Western meals. *4 Robinson Rd., tel. 2868–0828, fax 2868–1551, www.asiatravel.com/hongkong/bishoplei. 122 rooms, 81 suites. Restaurant, in-room data ports, minibars, pool, gym, laundry service, business services. AE, DC, MC, V.*

$ GARDEN VIEW INTERNATIONAL HOUSE. ★ This attractive, cylindrical guest house is on a hill overlooking the botanical gardens and harbor. Well-designed rooms make excellent use of irregular shapes and emphasize the picture windows. The coffee shop serves European and Asian dishes. You can use the swimming pool and gym at the adjoining YWCA. Garden View is a five-minute drive (Bus 12A or Minibus 1A) from Central and just a few minutes from the Peak tram station. *1 MacDonnell Rd., tel. 2877–3737, fax 2845–6263, www.ywca.org.hk. 130 rooms and suites. Coffee shop, pool, in-room data ports, kitchenettes (some), minibars, laundry service, business services. AE, DC, MC, V.*

WANCHAI

$$$$ GRAND HYATT. ★ "Grand" is the key word here. The ceiling of the art deco–style lobby was hand-painted by Italian artist Paola Dindo. Rooms are modern and well-designed. Each has a fax machine and Internet TV. Restaurants Grissini and Cantonese One Harbour Road are notable, as is the nightclub, JJ's. A decadent breakfast buffet is served on the ground floor. The Wanchai Star Ferry is nearby, but main walkways are slightly removed. *1 Harbour Rd., tel. 2588–1234, fax 2802–0677, www.hongkong.hyatt.com. 519 rooms, 51 suites. 4 restaurants, bar, in-room data ports, in-room safes,* minibars, room service, pool, hair salon, driving range, 2 tennis courts, gym, nightclub, dry cleaning, laundry service, concierge. AE, DC, MC, V.

$$$ CENTURY. Business travelers are well-served at this 23-story hotel. It's a 5-minute walk by covered overpass from the convention center and the MTR. Rooms are modern. The complex houses a popular Shanghainese restaurant, a 24-hour coffee shop, and a karaoke lounge. *238 Jaffe Rd., tel. 2598–8888, fax 2598–8866, www. century-hongkong-hotel.com. 497 rooms, 19 suites. 2 restaurants, 2 bars, coffee shop, in-room data ports, in-room safes, minibars, no-smoking floor, room service, pool, health club, shop, dry cleaning, laundry service, concierge, business services. AE, DC, MC, V.*

$$$ LUK KWOK. Hong Kong's leading architect, Remo Riva, designed this contemporary building. Luk Kwok's appeal is its proximity to the Hong Kong Convention & Exhibition Centre, the Academy for Performing Arts, and the Arts Centre. Guest rooms are clean and simple, with contemporary furniture; higher floors afford mountain or city views. It has a good Chinese restaurant. *72 Gloucester Rd., tel. 2866–2166, fax 2866–2622, www.lukkwokhotel.com. 191 rooms, 5 suites. 2 restaurants, lounge, in-room data ports, in-room safes, minibars, no-smoking floor, room service, laundry service, business services. AE, DC, MC, V.*

$$$ RENAISSANCE HARBOUR VIEW. Rooms at this attractive hotel are medium-size and modern, with fax machines and plenty of beveled-glass mirrors. Rooms on the executive floors have large desks. More than half the rooms overlook the harbor. Outdoor amenities include the largest hotel pool in town, gardens, and jogging trails. One of the best easy-listening jazz bands in town performs in the lobby lounge. *1 Harbour Rd., tel. 2802–8888, fax 2802–8833, www.renaissancehotels.com/HKGHV. 807 rooms, 53 suites. 4 restaurants, 2 bars, in-room data ports, in-room safes, minibars, 16 no-smoking floors, room service, pool, barbershop, hair salon, health club, 4 tennis courts, dry cleaning, laundry service, concierge, business services. AE, DC, MC, V.*

$–$$ HARBOUR VIEW INTERNATIONAL HOUSE. This waterfront YMCA property offers small but clean accommodations near the Wanchai

Star Ferry pier. The best rooms face the harbor. Both the Arts Centre and Academy for Performing Arts are next door. The hostel provides free shuttle service to Causeway Bay and the Central Star Ferry. Guests can use the superb YMCA Kowloon facilities, just a short ferry ride away, for a small fee. *4 Harbour Rd., tel. 2802–0111, fax 2802–9063. 320 rooms. Restaurant, no-smoking floor, laundry service. AE, DC, MC, V.*

$–$$ **THE WESLEY.** This 21-story hotel is a short walk from the Hong Kong Convention & Exhibition Centre, the Academy for Performing Arts, and the MTR. Rooms are small but pleasant; spacious corner "suites" have alcove work areas. You can use the health club in Wesley's sister Grand Plaza Hotel, in Quarry Bay, for a discounted fee. *22 Hennessy Rd., tel. 2866–6688, fax 2866–6613, www.grandhotel.com.hk/wesley. 251 rooms. Restaurant, no-smoking floor, laundry service, business services. AE, DC, MC, V.*

CAUSEWAY BAY

$$$$ **REGAL HONGKONG HOTEL.** Over-the-top decor in this hotel leans toward European, with marble floors, high windows, Louis XIV furniture, and gilded elevators. Rooms have spacious baths with triangular tubs. The sumptuous top-floor restaurant has great views of Victoria Park. The rooftop pool and terrace allow escape from the surrounding chaos. *88 Yee Wo St., tel. 2890–6633; 800/222–8888 in the U.S., fax 2881–0777, www.regalhongkong.com. 393 rooms, 32 suites. 6 restaurants, bar, in-room data ports, in-room safes, minibars, no-smoking floor, room service, pool, health club, shops, dry cleaning, laundry service, concierge, business services. AE, DC, MC, V.*

$$$ **THE EXCELSIOR.** One of Hong Kong's most popular hotels, the
★ Excelsior has spacious and clean rooms, many with splendid sea views. Hear live music at top-floor ToTT's Asian Grill & Bar. Tennis courts are on the roof, and there's a jogging track in adjacent Victoria Park. The hotel sits on the first plot of land auctioned by the British government when Hong Kong became a colony in 1841. *281 Gloucester Rd., tel. 2894–8888, fax 2895–6459,*

www.mandarin-oriental.com/excelsior. 866 rooms, 21 suites. 6 restaurants, 2 bars, in-room data ports, in-room safes, minibars, no-smoking floor, room service, hair salon, 2 tennis courts, health club, shop, dry cleaning, laundry service, concierge, business services. AE, DC, MC, V.

$$–$$$ PARK LANE. This elegant hotel overlooks Victoria Park and backs onto Causeway Bay. All rooms have luxurious marble bathrooms, handcrafted furniture, and marvelous views. The rooftop restaurant has a panoramic view and serves international cuisine. You can get some exercise walking the two-floor shopping arcade. 310 Gloucester Rd., tel. 2293–8888, fax 2576–7853, www.parklane.com.hk. 759 rooms, 33 suites. 2 restaurants, bar, in-room data ports, in-room safes, minibars, no-smoking floor, room service, hair salon, health club, shop, dry cleaning, laundry service, concierge, business services. AE, DC, MC, V.

$ NEW CATHAY. Fairly basic, this hotel is favored by Chinese tour groups. The small rooms have basic amenities; a Chinese seafood restaurant is on the top floor. Bustling Causeway Bay is just a few minutes away. 17 Tung Lo Wan Rd., tel. 2577–8211, fax 2576–9365, newcathay.gdhotels.net. 219 rooms, 3 suites. 2 restaurants, in-room safes, minibars, room service, laundry service. AE, DC, MC, V.

HAPPY VALLEY

$$ EMPEROR HAPPY VALLEY. It caters mainly to business and corporate travelers, but the Emperor is also the best deal in town for horse-racing fans—the racetrack is just a few minutes away by foot. Causeway Bay is 10 minutes by taxi. Rooms are clean. 1A Wang Tak St., tel. 2893–3693, fax 2834–6700, www.emperor-hv-hotel.com.hk. 157 rooms, 1 suite. 2 restaurants, bar, in-room safes, minibars, no-smoking floor, room service, laundry service. AE, DC, MC, V.

NORTH POINT

$$ CENTURY INN NORTH POINT. One of the newest hotels in the area, Century Inn is targeted toward the budget-minded who want to stay Hong Kong side. Many rooms have harbor views, compensating for their small size. 136–142 Java Rd., tel. 2204–6618, fax 2204–6677, www.centuryhotels.com. 202 rooms, 1 suite. 2 restaurants, lounge, in-room data ports, minibars, room service, pool, laundry service, business services. AE, DC, MC, V.

$$ NEWTON. In a boxy high-rise, this hotel close to an MTR station and has an on-site restaurant-bar with live entertainment. The Old Hong Kong Restaurant, in the basement, is popular. Rooms are small but adequate. 218 Electric Rd., tel. 2807–2333, fax 2807–1221, www.newtonhk.com. 362 rooms, 9 suites. 2 restaurants, bar, coffee shop, in-room data ports, minibars, room service, pool, sauna, laundry service, business services. AE, DC, MC, V.

QUARRY BAY

$$ GRAND PLAZA. Part of a large residential–commercial–entertainment complex, the rooms here are a little out of the way, but the hotel connects to the Taikoo MTR station and has a vast recreational club. It also has plenty of shopping in the adjoining Jusco department store. 2 Kornhill Rd., tel. 2886–0011, fax 2886–1738, www.grandhotel.com.hk/grandplaza. 208 rooms, 40 suites. 2 restaurants, in-room data ports, minibars, room service, indoor pool, miniature golf, tennis court, health club, badminton, squash, billiards, laundry service, business services. AE, DC, MC, V.

KOWLOON

HUNG HOM

$$$ HARBOUR PLAZA. Slightly off the beaten path, this opulent hotel has a unique harbor view from Wanchai to the South China Sea. Shuttles depart to and from Tsim Sha Tsui all day long; the Kowloon–Canton Railway station is 5 minutes away. Rooms are large, comfortable, and contemporary. Dining options include a Japanese *robatayaki* barbecue, a Cantonese restaurant, a grill, and a pub. 20 Tak Fung St., tel. 2621–3188, fax 2621–3311, www.harbour-plaza.com/hphk/. 381 rooms, 30 suites. 4 restaurants, pub, in-room data ports, in-room safes, minibars, room service, pool, hair salon,

kowloon lodging

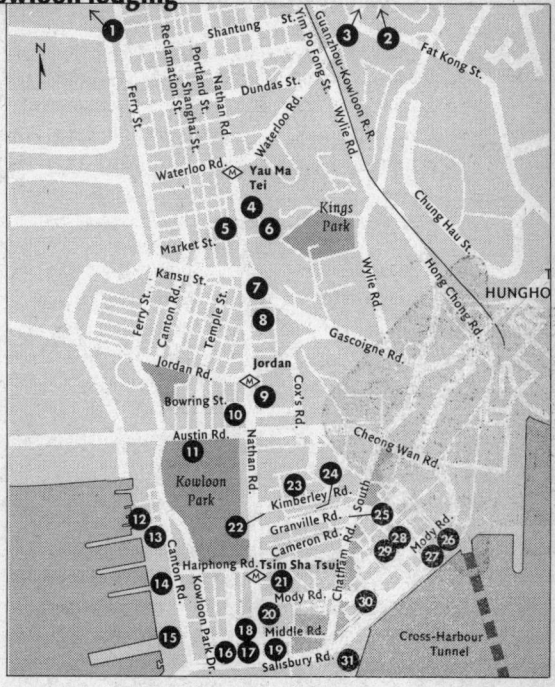

Booth Lodge, 4
BP International House, 11
Caritas Bianchi Lodge, 6
Concourse, 1
Dorsett Seaview, 5
Eaton, 7
Grand Stanford Inter-Continental, 27
Holiday Inn Golden Mile, 20
Inter-Continental Hong Kong, 32
Kimberley, 24
Kowloon, 18
Kowloon Shangri-La, 30
Majestic, 8
Marco Polo Hongkong, 15
Marco Polo Gateway, 14
Marco Polo Prince, 13
Metropole, 3
Miramar, 22
New Astor, 21
New World Renaissance, 31
Nikko, 26
Peninsula, 17
Pruton Prudential, 9
Ramada Hotel Kowloon, 25
Regal Kowloon, 28
Royal Garden, 29
Royal Pacific Hotel & Towers, 12
Royal Plaza, 2
Salisbury YMCA, 16
Shamrock, 10
Sheraton Hong Kong Hotel and Towers, 19
Windsor, 23

spa, health club, shop, dry cleaning, laundry service, concierge, business services. AE, DC, MC, V.

$ HOLY CARPENTER GUEST HOUSE. Occupying space in a community center that also houses a church, this small hostel is a 10-minute walk from the Kowloon–Canton Railway station. Don't expect more than a humble room and very small bathroom. Reserve at least a month in advance. *1 Dyer Ave., tel. 2362–0301, fax 2362–2193. 14 rooms. MC, V.*

TSIM SHA TSUI

$$$$ ★ INTER-CONTINENTAL HONG KONG. World-class style and innovation are coupled some of the best views in Hong Kong. Spacious, bright, and sophisticated rooms have Internet TV and sunken marble baths; most suites have a steam shower. The five restaurants include the high-profile Yü, serving spectacular seafood; Plume, with contemporary European cuisine; and the Steak House. *18 Salisbury Rd., tel. 2721–1211; 800/545–4000 in the U.S., fax 2739–4546, www.interconti.com. 510 rooms, 92 suites. 5 restaurants, pool, spa, health club, shop, dry cleaning, laundry service, concierge, business services. AE, DC, MC, V.*

$$$$ ★ PENINSULA. A worldwide legend, this 1928 hotel has colonial architecture, a fleet of Rolls-Royces, attentive room valets, and daily high tea. Helicopter sightseeing tours depart from the roof. Rooms have fax machines and bedside remotes that operate everything from the lights to the curtains. Huge corner rooms have glorious views of the skyline. The hotel has an exclusive shopping arcade and the hippest of the hip rooftop restaurants, Felix. *Salisbury Rd., tel. 2366–6251, fax 2722–4170, fasttrack.hongkong.peninsula.com. 246 rooms, 54 suites. 7 restaurants, bar, in-room data ports, in-room safes, minibars, room service, pool, hair salon, spa, health club, shops, dry cleaning, laundry service, concierge, business services, helipad. AE, DC, MC, V.*

$$$$ SHERATON HONG KONG HOTEL AND TOWERS. At the southern end of the Golden Mile, the Sheraton is contemporary, even avant-garde. Guest rooms have harbor, city, or courtyard views. Reach the rooftop pool and terrace via the exterior glass elevator. The sky lounge has a terrific harbor view, Someplace Else is a popular at happy hour, and the delightful Oyster & Wine Bar is on the top floor. *20 Nathan Rd., tel. 2369–1111, fax 2739–8707, www.sheraton.com. 686 rooms, 94 suites. 5 restaurants, 3 lounges, in-room data ports, in-room safes, minibars, 2 no-smoking floors, room service, pool, health club, shop, dry cleaning, laundry service, concierge, business services. AE, DC, MC, V.*

$$$–$$$$ HOLIDAY INN GOLDEN MILE. In the hub of Kowloon's business and shopping area, this business-style hotel is a steady favorite. Rooms here are small and nondescript but windows on the facade have sweeping views of Nathan Road, and the Avenue restaurant serves delicious contemporary European cuisine on the third floor, overlooking Tsim Sha Tsui's main artery. *50 Nathan Rd., tel. 2369–3111, fax 2369–8016, www.goldenmile.com. 592 rooms, 8 suites. 3 restaurants, bar, lounge, in-room data ports, in-room safes, minibars, 7 no-smoking floors, room service, pool, health club, shop, dry cleaning, laundry service, business services. AE, DC, MC, V.*

$$$–$$$$ MARCO POLO HONGKONG. A prominent and outrageous Oktoberfest is held at this hotel next to the Star Ferry. The complex houses offices, shopping malls, movie theaters, and restaurants. It feels a bit dated, but personal comfort is a priority. Miniature bathrobes, mild shampoos, and rubber ducks are provided for tots. *Harbour City, Canton Rd., tel. 2113–0088, fax 2113–0011, www.marcopolohotels.com/thehongkonghotel/index.html. 621 rooms, 44 suites. 6 restaurants, lounge, in-room data ports, in-room safes, minibars, 2 no-smoking floors, room service, pool, barbershop, hair salon, dry cleaning, laundry service, concierge, business services. AE, DC, MC, V.*

$$$ MARCO POLO GATEWAY. This hotel in the shopping and commercial area along Canton Road is close to the MTR station. Rooms and suites have large windows and comfortable beds.

The most notable restaurant is La Brasserie. The staff is well-trained. You can use the pool at the nearby Marco Polo Hongkong. *Harbour City, Canton Rd., tel. 2113–0888, fax 2113–0022, www.marcopolohotels.com/marco-frame.html. 384 rooms, 56 suites. 3 restaurants, bar, in-room data ports, in-room safes, minibars, 3 no-smoking floors, room service, barbershop, dry cleaning, laundry service, business services. AE, DC, MC, V.*

$$$ **MARCO POLO PRINCE.** Convenient to upscale shops and cinemas, Tsim Sha Tsui, and the China Hong Kong Terminal, this hotel has mostly small, comfortable rooms that overlook expansive Kowloon Park; some suites have views of Victoria Harbour. The Spice Market restaurant serves Southeast Asian buffets. You can use the pool at the Marco Polo Hongkong, a 5-minute walk away. *Harbour City, Canton Rd., tel. 2113–1888, fax 2113–0066, www.marcopolohotels.com/prince. 345 rooms, 51 suites. Restaurant, bar, deli, in-room data ports, in-room safes, minibars, no-smoking floor, room service, shop, dry cleaning, laundry service, business services. AE, DC, MC, V.*

$$$ **NEW WORLD RENAISSANCE.** This popular lodging is part of a large shopping complex and has magnificent views of Hong Kong Island. Rooms are modern and spacious, with a homey feel. Greenery surrounds the outdoor pool. Among the three restaurants, the Panorama has one of the best harbor views in town. *22 Salisbury Rd., tel. 2369–4111, fax 2369–9387, www.renaissancehotels.com. 501 rooms, 42 suites. 3 restaurants, lounge, in-room data ports, in-room safes, minibars, 4 no-smoking floors, room service, pool, hair salon, health club, dry cleaning, laundry service, business services. AE, DC, MC, V.*

$$–$$$ **MIRAMAR.** Hong Kong's first post–World War II hotel, Miramar was originally intended as a shelter for missionaries expelled from China. The vast lobby has a stained-glass ceiling, rooms are functional, and service is friendly. Two Chinese restaurants and a microbrewery are adjacent in the shopping center. Two MTR stations are nearby. *130 Nathan Rd., tel. 2368–1111, fax 2369–1788. 512 rooms, 13 suites. 3 restaurants, bar, no-smoking floor, indoor pool, shop, dry cleaning, laundry service, business services, meeting rooms. AE, DC, MC, V.*

$$ BP INTERNATIONAL HOUSE. Rooms at this hotel built by the Boy Scouts Association have panoramic views of Victoria Harbour. A hall hosts exhibitions, conventions, and concerts; the health club is one of the biggest in town. *8 Austin Rd., tel. 2376–1111, fax 2376–1333, www.megahotels.com.hk. 524 rooms, 11 suites. 2 restaurants, health club, coin laundry, business services, parking (fee). AE, DC, MC, V.*

$$ KIMBERLEY. On one of the colorfully busy streets between Nathan Road and Tsim Sha Tsui East, this hotel offers plenty of bright, clean rooms. Its health spa offers masseurs. Golf driving nets are available. The two main restaurants serve Cantonese and Japanese cuisines. *28 Kimberley Rd., tel. 2723–3888, fax 2723–1318, www.kimberley.com.hk. 497 rooms, 49 suites. 3 restaurants, bar, in-room data ports, minibars, room service, spa, health club, laundry service, business services. AE, DC, MC, V.*

$$ KOWLOON. ★ Kowloon means "nine dragons" in Chinese, and at this shimmering, high-tech hotel, the triangular windows and lobby ceiling—made from hundreds of hand-blown Venetian-glass pyramids—represent dragons' teeth. You can use some of the services at the adjacent Peninsula hotel for a fee. Rooms are small, but each has a fax machine and Internet TV with CD-ROM drive. The Kowloon is next to the Tsim Sha Tsui MTR and minutes from the Star Ferry. *19–21 Nathan Rd., tel. 2929–2888, fax 2739–9811, fasttrack.kowloon.peninsula.com. 719 rooms, 17 suites. 3 restaurants, in-room data ports, minibars, 5 no-smoking floors, room service, hair salon, shop, dry cleaning, laundry service, business services. AE, DC, MC, V.*

$$ RAMADA HOTEL KOWLOON. This hotel has a cozy atmosphere; there's a fireplace in the lobby and comfortable rooms have natural wood furnishings. The bar attracts young locals for drinks and karaoke. *73–75 Chatham Rd., South Tsim Sha Tsui, tel. 2311–1100, fax 2311–6000, www.ramadahotels.com. 203 rooms, 2 suites. Restaurant, bar, in-room safes, minibars, room service, laundry service, business services. AE, DC, MC, V.*

$–$$ NEW ASTOR. Small and inviting, this triangular hotel is on a busy corner of Old Tsim Sha Tsui across from the MTR. Rooms have dark wood furniture. New Astor attracts groups from China and more affluent backpackers. Granville Road is a short walk. *11 Carnarvon Rd., tel. 2366–7261, fax 2722–7122, www.newastor.com.hk. 147 rooms, 1 suite. Restaurant, in-room safes, minibars, room service, shop, laundry service, business services. AE, DC, MC, V.*

$–$$ **ROYAL PACIFIC HOTEL & TOWERS.** On the Tsim Sha Tsui waterfront, the Royal Pacific is part of the Hong Kong China City complex, which also houses the ferry terminal to China. Guest rooms are small but attractive. The hotel connects to Kowloon Park by a footbridge. *33 Canton Rd., tel. 2736–1188, fax 2736–1212, www.royalpacific.com.hk. 641 rooms, 32 suites. 3 restaurants, bar, in-room data ports, in-room safes, minibars, room service, health club, squash, dry cleaning, laundry service, business services. AE, DC, MC, V.*

$–$$ **WINDSOR.** This humble but smart hotel offers clean accommodations just east of the Golden Mile. Business services include secretarial support. When taking a cab here, be sure to say "Windsor hotel," as the Windsor Cinema and the Windsor House are more widely known. *39–43A Kimberley Rd., tel. 2739–5665, fax 2311–5101, www.windsorhotel.com.hk. 165 rooms, 1 suite. 2 restaurants, bar, in-room data ports, minibars, room service, laundry service, business services. AE, DC, MC, V.*

$ ★ **SALISBURY YMCA.** In Hong Kong, YMCAs tend to far surpass Ys elsewhere, and this five-star hotel is no exception, with clean rooms, superb health facilities, and the same magnificent harbor view as the Pen. It also has a beautiful garden, a conference room, and a children's library. In-house movies are free. The restaurants serve good, cheap Chinese food. *41 Salisbury Rd., tel. 2369–2211, fax 2739–9315, www.ymcahk.org.hk. 303 rooms, 62 suites. 2 restaurants, lounge, in-room data ports, in-room safes, room service, indoor pool, hair salon, health club, squash, shop, coin laundry, meeting room. AE, DC, MC, V.*

TSIM SHA TSUI EAST

$$$$ KOWLOON SHANGRI-LA. ★ Business travelers are pampered at this upscale hotel. Rooms have fax machines and free newspaper delivery, and to keep you on schedule, elevator carpets change with the day of the week. Fairly large and modern, the rooms have views of the harbor or city. The restaurants have magnificent views. The lounge and Blue Note bar provide live entertainment. *64 Mody Rd., tel. 2721–2111; 800/942–5050 in the U.S., fax 2723–8686, www.shangri-la.com/eng. 705 rooms, 25 suites. 5 restaurants, bar, lounge, in-room data ports, in-room safes, minibars, no-smoking floor, room service, indoor pool, barbershop, health club, dry cleaning, laundry service, concierge, business services. AE, DC, MC, V.*

$$$ GRAND STANFORD INTER-CONTINENTAL. More than half the rooms at this luxury hotel have an unobstructed harbor view. The staff is friendly, and the rooms are modern and comfortable. Well-known restaurants include Mistral and Tiffany's New York Bar, where entertainers sing popular American songs. *70 Mody Rd., tel. 2721–5161, fax 2732–2233, www.grandstanford.com. 554 rooms, 25 suites. 4 restaurants, bar, in-room data ports, in-room safes, minibars, room service, pool, health club, shop, dry cleaning, laundry service, business services. AE, DC, MC, V.*

$$$ NIKKO. At the far end of Tsim Sha Tsui East, this luxury harborfront hotel attracts mostly Japanese tourists. The spacious premises are clean but a bit dated. Nearly 200 rooms enjoy harbor views. The popular restaurant Sagano is Japanese. *72 Mody Rd., tel. 2739–1111, fax 2311–3122, www.hotelnikko.com.hk. 444 rooms, 17 suites. 4 restaurants, 3 bars, in-room data ports (some), in-room safes, minibars, room service, pool, health club, shop, business services. AE, DC, MC, V.*

$$$ ROYAL GARDEN. A lush garden atrium with running water rises from the ground level of this hotel to the rooftop. There's a sense of serenity here, and all of the spacious rooms surround the atrium. Sabatini is a sister to the famous Roman restaurant, and the rooftop health club is state-of-the-art. The pool, open year-round, is fashioned after an ancient Roman bath, with fountains and underwater music. 69 Mody Rd., tel. 2721–5215, fax 2369–9976, www.theroyalgardenhotel.com.hk. 374 rooms, 48 suites. 4 restaurants, bar, in-room data ports, in-room safes, minibars, no-smoking floor, room service, indoor-outdoor pool, hair salon, spa, tennis court, health club, shop, dance club, dry cleaning, laundry service, concierge, business services. AE, DC, MC, V.

$$ **REGAL KOWLOON.** French-inspired, this hotel has rooms with Louis XVI–style furniture and an impressive lobby tapestry. Rooms on the club floors have a more minimalist modern appeal. The French restaurant Maman serves home-style French cooking in a relaxed setting. 71 Mody Rd., tel. 2722–1818, fax 2369–6950, www.regalkowloon.com. 564 rooms, 34 suites. 4 restaurants, 2 bars, in-room data ports, in-room safes, minibars, no-smoking floor, room service, hair salon, health club, shop, dry cleaning, laundry service, concierge, business services. AE, DC, MC, V.

YAU MA TEI AND MONG KOK

$$ **CONCOURSE.** One of Hong Kong's nicer budget hotels, the Concourse is tucked away from Nathan Road but still only a minute's walk from the Prince Edward MTR station. The hotel is well placed for a glimpse of real, day-to-day life, amid coffeehouses, noodle shops, and active nightlife options. The hotel has Chinese and pan-Asian restaurants. 22 Lai Chi Kok Rd., Mong Kok, tel. 2397–6683, fax 2381–3768, www.hotelconcourse.com.hk. 425 rooms, 5 suites. 2 restaurants, bar, coffee shop, in-room data ports, minibars, room service, laundry service, business services. AE, DC, MC, V.

$$ **EATON.** Housed in a brick-red shopping and cinema complex on Nathan Road, Eaton is a stone's throw from Temple Street, the busy night market that bustles with vendors, fortune-tellers, and Chinese opera singers. Rooms are clean and modern. 380 Nathan Rd., Yau Ma Tei, tel. 2782–1818, fax 2782–5563, www.eaton-hotel.com. 458 rooms, 30 suites. 6 restaurants, bar, in-room data ports, minibars, no-smoking floor, room service, pool, gym, laundry service, business services. AE, DC, MC, V.

$$ MAJESTIC. On the site of the old Majestic Cinema on upper Nathan Road, this hotel has sparsely furnished rooms with contemporary furnishings. All suites have fax machines. Facilities are minimal, but the complex has shops and a cinema. Plenty of restaurants and the MTR are nearby. *348 Nathan Rd., Yau Ma Tei, tel. 2781–1333, fax 2781–1773, www.majestichotel.com.hk. 387 rooms, 9 suites. Bar, coffee shop, in-room data ports, minibars, no-smoking floor, room service, shop, cinema, laundry service, business services. AE, DC, MC, V.*

$$ PRUTON PRUDENTIAL. A real find for bargain-hunters, this hotel rises from a busy corner above the Jordan MTR station. Spacious rooms have views of bustling Nathan Road and there are five executive floors. The hotel shares a building with a lively shopping mall. *222 Nathan Rd., Yau Ma Tei, tel. 2311–8222, fax 2311–1304. 415 rooms, 17 suites. Bar, coffee shop, in-room data ports, minibars, room service, pool, shop, laundry service, business services. AE, DC, MC, V.*

$–$$ DORSETT SEAVIEW. Convenient to the Yau Ma Tei MTR, this hotel is on Shanghai Street, where traditional Hong Kong thrives. Temple Street is nearby, as is the art-house cinema, Broadway Cinematheque. The restaurant has bargain-priced buffets, especially for lunch. Rooms are very small. *268 Shanghai St., Yau Ma Tei, tel. 2782–0882, fax 2388–1803, www.dorsettseaview.com.hk. 254 rooms, 3 suites. Restaurant, bar, lounge, minibars, room service, laundry service. AE, DC, MC, V.*

$–$$ METROPOLE. A harmonious mélange of East and West, Metropole has simple and clean rooms, and is just north of Nathan Road's major shopping area. The on-site Chinese restaurant, House of Tang, is locally renowned for its master chefs, who serve authentic Szechuan and Cantonese food. *75 Waterloo Rd., Yau Ma Tei, tel. 2761–1711, fax 2761–0769, www.metropole.com.hk. 479 rooms, 8 suites. 3 restaurants, bar, in-room data ports, minibars, room service, pool, health club, laundry service, business services. AE, DC, MC, V.*

$–$$ ROYAL PLAZA. One of Hong Kong's newer additions, the Royal Plaza is easily accessible from either the adjacent Kowloon–Canton Railway station or the nearby MTR station. It is part of the

Hotel How-Tos

Where you stay does make a difference. Do you prefer a modern high-rise or an intimate B&B? A center-city location or the quiet suburbs? What facilities do you want? Sort through your priorities, then price it all out.

HOW TO GET A DEAL After you've chosen a likely candidate or two, phone them directly and price a room for your travel dates. Then call the hotel's toll-free number and ask the same questions. Also try consolidators and hotel-room discounters. You won't hear the same rates twice. On the spot, make a reservation as soon as you are quoted a price you want to pay.

PROMISES, PROMISES If you have special requests, make them when you reserve. Get written confirmation of any promises.

SETTLE IN Upon arriving, make sure everything works—lights and lamps, TV and radio, sink, tub, shower, and anything else that matters. Report any problems immediately. And don't wait until you need extra pillows or blankets or an ironing board to call housekeeping. Also check out the fire emergency instructions. Know where to find the fire exits, and make sure your companions do, too.

IF YOU NEED TO COMPLAIN Be polite but firm. Explain the problem to the person in charge. Suggest a course of action. If you aren't satisfied, repeat your requests to the manager. Document everything: Take pictures and keep a written record of who you've spoken with, when, and what was said. Contact your travel agent, if he made the reservations.

KNOW THE SCORE When you go out, take your hotel's business cards (one for everyone in your party). If you have extras, you can give them out to new acquaintances who want to call you.

TIP UP FRONT For special services, a tip or partial tip in advance can work wonders.

USE ALL THE HOTEL RESOURCES A concierge can make difficult things easy. But a desk clerk, bellhop, or other hotel employee who's friendly, smart, and ambitious can often steer you straight as well. A gratuity is in order if the advice is helpful.

massive New Century Place shopping complex, and its facilities include a ballroom and a 40-m pool with underwater music. The garden allows peace and quiet. *193 Prince Edward Rd. W, Mong Kok, tel. 2928–8822, fax 2628–3383, www.royalplaza.com.hk. 419 rooms, 50 suites. 3 restaurants, bar, in-room data ports, in-room safes, minibars, room service, indoor pool, spa, health club, laundry service, business services. AE, DC, MC, V.*

$ **BOOTH LODGE.** This pleasant contemporary retreat is down a dead-end side street. Everything in the renovated lodge is clean, bright, and new, from freshly painted walls to starched sheets on the double beds. The coffee shop serves mainly buffets, and has an outdoor balcony with nice views. The Yau Ma Tei MTR is nearby. *11 Wing Sing La., Yau Ma Tei, tel. 2771–9266, fax 2385–1140. 54 rooms. Coffee shop, laundry service. AE, MC, V.*

$ **CARITAS BIANCHI LODGE.** Clean and friendly, this hostel has simple decor and basic facilities—including private bathrooms. Despite its proximity to busy Nathan Road and the Jade and Temple Street markets, it remains fairly quiet and peaceful. *4 Cliff Rd., Yau Ma Tei, tel. 2388–1111, fax 2770–6669. 88 rooms, 2 suites. Restaurant, minibars, laundry service. AE, DC, MC, V.*

$ **SHAMROCK.** At this writing, Shamrock was busy sprucing itself up with refurbished rooms, lobby, and facade. It is in the middle of all the Yau Ma Tei action, just north of Kowloon Park and steps from the Jordan MTR. Rooms are a decent size, and the hotel offers buffet-style dining. *223 Nathan Rd., Yau Ma Tei, tel. 2735–2271, fax 2736–7354, www.asiatravel.com/shamrock. 128 rooms, 19 suites. Restaurant, in-room data ports, minibars, room service, laundry service. AE, DC, MC, V.*

practical information

Air Travel

CARRIERS

➤ **MAJOR AIRLINES: Asiana** (tel. 800/227–4262). **Canadian** (tel. 800/426–7000). **Cathay Pacific Airways** (tel. 800/233–2742 in the U.S.; 800/268–6868 in Canada). **China Airlines** (tel. 800/227–5118). **Continental** (tel. 800/231–0856). **Korean Air** (tel. 800/438–5000). **Northwest** (tel. 800/447–4747). **Qantas** (tel. 800/227–4500). **Singapore Airlines** (tel. 800/742–3333). **United Airlines** (tel. 800/241–6522). **Virgin Atlantic** (tel. 800/862–8621).

➤ **FROM THE U.K.: British Airways** (tel. 0845/77–33–77). **Cathay Pacific Airways** (tel. 020/7747–8888). **Virgin Atlantic** (tel. 01293/747–747).

CHECK-IN & BOARDING

Always ask your carrier about its check-in policy. Plan to arrive at the airport about two hours before your scheduled departure time for domestic flights and 2½ to 3 hours before international flights. The first to get bumped are passengers who checked in late and those flying on discounted tickets, so **get to the gate and check in as early as possible**, especially during peak periods.

If you plan on taking the train to the Hong Kong International Airport at Chek Lap Kok, **check your luggage at the Airport Express Railway station** on Hong Kong Island. You must check in at least three hours in advance for this efficient, time-saving service.

Remember to **retain your Hong Kong entry slip** that the customs official gives you at passport control. You will need to return this paper when you present your passport for your return trip home.

RECONFIRMING

If you are flying on a mainland Chinese airline, you must reconfirm your ticket at least 24 hours before leaving Hong Kong or risk losing your seat. You can have your travel agent do this for you.

Airports & Transfers

The gateway to Hong Kong is the sleek and sophisticated Hong Kong International Airport at Chek Lap Kok, universally known only as Chek Lap Kok. Remember to hold onto HK$50 for the airport tax, payable on departure from the country. It is only levied on those 12 years and older and is waived for all transit and transfer passengers who arrive and leave on the same day. Smoking is not permitted within the airport (the fine is HK$1,000) or on the Airport Express Railway.

➤ **AIRPORT INFORMATION: Hong Kong International Airport** (tel. 852/2181–0000).

AIRPORT TRANSFERS

The spectacular, high-speed, high-frequency Airport Express Railway whisks passengers between the airport and Kowloon in 19 minutes, and to and from Hong Kong Island (Central) in 23 minutes. Airport Express has convenient in-town check-in, whereby you **check your luggage, get your boarding pass, and pay departure tax while still on Hong Kong Island**. To do this, you must purchase an Airport Express ticket and get to the train station at least three hours before your flight; the office is open 6 AM–1 AM. The Airport Express station is connected to the MTR's Central station (albeit via a long, underground walkway with no luggage carts). One-way fare to or from Central is HK$70; from Kowloon, HK$60.

The Airport Express also runs a free shuttle bus between major hotels and its Hong Kong or Kowloon stations. To board, you must show your ticket, boarding pass, or Airport Express ticket. Airbus has eight routes covering just about every hotel and hostel in Hong Kong and Kowloon. Prices range from HK$20 to HK$45 for the one-hour trip. A 24-hour Airport Shuttle bus departs major hotels every 30 minutes and costs HK$120.

A number of regular public buses—including Cityflyer, Kowloon Motor Bus, and Long Wing Bus Company—serve the airport; though cheaper (HK$23 and under), these take longer than express options. Taxis from the airport cost up to HK$400 for Hong Kong Island destinations and up to HK$320 for Kowloon destinations, plus HK$5 per piece of luggage. DCH Limo Service is located at Kiosk 4 in the Arrival Hall. Limo rides from the airport range from HK$450 to HK$600.

➤ **TAXIS & SHUTTLES: Airbus** (tel. 2745–4466). **Airport Express Rail** (tel. 2881–8888). **Airport Shuttle** (tel. 2377–0733). **Cityflyer** (tel. 2873–0818). **DCH Limo Service** (tel. 2262–1888, fax 2753–6768). **Kowloon Motor Bus** (tel. 2745–4466). **Long Wing Bus Company** (tel. 2786–6036).

Boat & Ferry Travel

The century-old Star Ferry is a Hong Kong landmark. Vessels connect Hong Kong Island with Kowloon in just eight minutes; the ride costs HK$2.20 upper deck, HK$1.70 lower deck. Ferries also run to and between Wanchai and Tsim Sha Tsui; both rides cost HK$5.

➤ **BOAT & FERRY INFORMATION: HKTB Visitor Hot Line** (tel. 2508–1234). **Star Ferry** (tel. 2366–2576 or 2845–2324).

Bus Travel Around Hong Kong

Double-decker buses run from 6 AM to midnight, and cover most parts of Hong Kong. Bus drivers usually don't speak English, so you may have to ask other passengers for help or you must know exactly where you want to disembark.

When determining bus direction, buses ending with the letter L will eventually connect to the Kowloon–Canton Railway; buses ending with the letter M connect to an MTR station; and buses ending with the letter X are express buses.

Maxicabs and minibuses, cream-colored buses that seat 16, are quick, though they cost slightly more than buses. Both can be waved down at any point.

For information, call the HKTB Visitor Hot Line or, for double-decker-bus route maps, stop in at the HKTB Information and Gift Centres at The Center, 99 Queen's Road Central in Central or at the Star Ferry Concourse in Kowloon.

➤ **BUS INFORMATION: HKTB Visitor Hot Line** (tel. 2508–1234).

PAYING

Double-decker bus fares range from HK$1.20 to HK$45; the fare is paid when entering the bus. Maxicab fares range from HK$1.50 to HK$18. Similarly, you pay as you board. Minibus fares range from HK$2 to HK$20, but you pay as you exit. You must use exact change.

Business Resources

BUSINESS CENTERS

Hong Kong supports many business centers outside hotels, and some are considerably cheaper than hotel facilities. Harbour International Business Centre provides typing, secretarial support, and office rentals. Reservations are not required.

➤ **BUSINESS CENTER INFORMATION: AMS Management Service Ltd.** (Wilson House, 19–27 Wyndham St., 18th floor, Central, tel. 2846–3100, fax 2810–7002). **Brauner's Business Centre** (Kowloon Centre, 29–43 Ashley Rd., Room 903–5, 9th floor, Tsim Sha Tsui, tel. 2376–2855, fax 2376–3360). **Business Executive Centre** (Kinwick Centre, 32 Hollywood Rd., 23rd floor, Central, tel. 2827–7322, fax 2827–4227). **Business Station** (Cosmos Bldg., 8–11 Lan Kwai Fong, 6th floor, Central, tel. 2523–6810, fax 2530–5071). **Central Executive Business Centre** (Central Bldg., 1 Pedder St., 11th floor, Central, tel. 2841–7888, fax 2810–1868). **Harbour International Business Centre** (2802 Admiralty Centre Tower I, 18 Harcourt Rd., tel. 2529–0356, fax 2861–3420).

➤ **CONVENTION CENTER: Hong Kong Convention and Exhibition Centre** (1 Expo Dr., Wanchai, Hong Kong Island, tel. 2582–8888, fax 2802–0000).

BUSINESS SERVICES

All hotels and business centers have photocopy machines, as do many stores. For heavy-duty, oversize, and color copying, try Xerox.

Inquire at the General Post Office (☞ Mail & Shipping) to see which post offices have fax service. Hong Kong Telecom International (HKTI) has one 24-hour office to handle public telephone, fax, and telex. Contact DHL if your business center or hotel does not offer messenger services.

➤ **COPY SERVICES: Xerox** (Central: New Henry House, 10 Ice House St., 2nd floor, tel. 2524–9799, fax 2845–9271; Admiralty: United Centre, Unit 34, 95 Queensway, 2nd floor, tel. 2527–6162, fax 2529–5416; Wanchai: Shanghai Ind. Investment Bldg., 58 Hennessy Rd., tel. 2528–0761, fax 2865–0799; Tsim Sha Tsui: China Hong Kong City, 33 Canton Rd., Shop 3, 2nd floor, tel. 2736–6011, fax 2736–6278).

➤ **FAX & MESSENGER SERVICES: DHL Express** (tel. 2765–8111). **HKTI** (Hermes House, 10 Middle Rd., Tsim Sha Tsui, Kowloon, tel. 2724–8322).

➤ **TRANSLATION SERVICES: CIAP Hong Kong** (2A, Tower 10, Pak Pat Shan, Red Hill, Hong Kong, tel. 2697–5114). **Polyglot**

Translations (14B Time Centre, 53 Hollywood Rd., Central, tel. 2851–7232). **Translation Business** (13D, Chinaweal Centre, 414–424 Jaffe Rd., Wanchai, tel. 2893–5000).

TRADE INFORMATION

➤ **CONTACTS: Hong Kong Trade Development Council** (Office Tower Convention Plaza, 1 Harbour Rd., 38th floor, tel. 2584–4333, fax 2824–0249). **Industry Department** (Ocean Centre, 5 Canton Rd., 14th floor, Kowloon, tel. 2737–2573, fax 2730–4633). **Trade Department** (Trade Department Tower, 700 Nathan Rd., Kowloon, tel. 2392–2922, fax 2789–2435).

Business Hours

Nearly all businesses, even tourist-related ones, will shut down for major holidays such as Chinese Lunar New Year, Christmas, and New Year's.

Banks are open weekdays 9–4:30 and Saturday 9–12:30. Cash machines are plentiful. Museums and sights are usually open six days a week from 9 to 5. Some are closed one day per week, usually Monday or Tuesday. Pharmacies are generally open from about 10 AM–9 PM. There are no 24-hour pharmacies. Stores are usually open from 10 AM until 9 or 9:30 PM. Office hours are more or less the same as in the West—9 to 5 or 6. Some offices close for lunch from 1 PM–2 PM.

Car Travel

The best advice we can give is **don't drive in Hong Kong**. In addition to the fact that gasoline and parking are prohibitively expensive, local bus and truck drivers are very aggressive, making it a difficult and dangerous city to drive in.

If you insist on driving here, remember in this former British colony, the road rules are drive on the left and signage is British symbols. Always remember to **look left before you cross the street.**

If you decide to rent a car, you may want to hire a driver as well; this can be arranged through your hotel.

Children in Hong Kong

SIGHTS & ATTRACTIONS
Places that are especially appealing to children are indicated by a rubber-duckie icon (🦆) in the margin.

SUPPLIES & EQUIPMENT
Baby supplies such as diapers are widely available throughout the city. A variety of brands of powdered milk, Heinz baby foods, Johnson & Johnson lotions and powders, and Gerber plastic nursers and silicone nipples are all readily found at supermarkets, or at pharmaceutical–cosmetics chain stores such as **Watson's** (tel. 2186–8595) or **Fanda Perfume Co., Ltd.** (tel. 2526–6623), which are scattered throughout Hong Kong.

TRANSPORTATION
Most public transportation services charge half price for children under 12.

Consumer Protection

Whenever shopping or buying travel services in Hong Kong, **pay with a major credit card**, if possible, so you can cancel payment or get reimbursed if there's a problem. Note, however, that this will often increase the price of your purchase by 3% to 5%. If you're doing business with a particular company for the first time, **contact your local Better Business Bureau and the attorney general's offices** in your state and (for U.S. businesses) the company's home state as well. Have any complaints been filed? Finally, if you're buying a package or tour, always **consider travel insurance** that includes default coverage.

➤ **BBBs: Council of Better Business Bureaus** (4200 Wilson Blvd., Suite 800, Arlington, VA 22203, tel. 703/276–0100, fax 703/525–8277, www.bbb.org).

Customs & Duties

When shopping, **keep receipts** for all purchases. Upon reentering the country, **be ready to show customs officials what you've bought.** If you feel a duty is incorrect or object to the way your clearance was handled, note the inspector's badge number and ask to see a supervisor. If the problem isn't resolved, write to the appropriate authorities, beginning with the port director at your point of entry.

IN AUSTRALIA

Australian residents who are 18 or older may bring home A$400 worth of souvenirs and gifts (including jewelry), 250 cigarettes or 250 grams of tobacco, and 1,125 ml of alcohol (including wine, beer, and spirits). Residents under 18 may bring back A$200 worth of goods. Prohibited items include meat products. Seeds, plants, and fruits need to be declared upon arrival.

➤ **INFORMATION: Australian Customs Service** (Regional Director, Box 8, Sydney, NSW 2001, Australia, tel. 02/9213–2000, fax 02/9213–4000, www.customs.gov.au).

IN CANADA

Canadian residents who have been out of Canada for at least seven days may bring home C$500 worth of goods duty-free. If you've been away fewer than seven days but more than 48 hours, the duty-free allowance drops to C$200; if your trip lasts 24–48 hours, the allowance is C$50. You may not pool allowances with family members. Goods claimed under the C$500 exemption may follow you by mail; those claimed under the lesser exemptions must accompany you. Alcohol and tobacco products may be included in the seven-day and 48-hour exemptions but not in the 24-hour exemption. If you meet the age requirements of the province or territory through which you reenter Canada, you may bring in, duty-free, 1.14 liters (40 imperial ounces) of wine or liquor or 24 12-ounce cans or bottles of beer or ale. If you are 16 or older you may bring in, duty-free, 200 cigarettes and 50 cigars. Check ahead of time with Revenue

Canada or the Department of Agriculture for policies regarding meat products, seeds, plants, and fruits.

You may send an unlimited number of gifts worth up to C$60 each duty-free to Canada. Label the package UNSOLICITED GIFT—VALUE UNDER $60. Alcohol and tobacco are excluded.

➤ **INFORMATION: Revenue Canada** (2265 St. Laurent Blvd. S, Ottawa, Ontario K1G 4K3, Canada, tel. 613/993–0534; 800/461–9999 in Canada, fax 613/991–4126, www.ccra-adrc.gc.ca).

IN HONG KONG

Except for the usual prohibitions against narcotics, explosives, firearms, and ammunition (all but narcotics must be declared upon arrival and handed over for safekeeping until departure), and modest limits on alcohol, tobacco products, and perfume, you can bring anything you want into Hong Kong, including an unlimited amount of money.

Nonresident visitors may bring in, duty-free, 200 cigarettes or 50 cigars or 250 grams of tobacco, and 1 liter of alcohol.

➤ **INFORMATION: Hong Kong Customs and Excise Department** (10/F, Canton Road Government Offices, 393 Canton Rd., Kowloon, tel. 2815–7711, fax 2542–3334, www.info.gov.hk/customs).

IN NEW ZEALAND

Homeward-bound residents 17 or older may bring back NZ$700 worth of souvenirs and gifts. Your duty-free allowance also includes 4.5 liters of wine or beer; one 1,125-ml bottle of spirits; and either 200 cigarettes, 250 grams of tobacco, 50 cigars, or a combination of the three up to 250 grams. Prohibited items include meat products, seeds, plants, and fruits.

➤ **INFORMATION: New Zealand Customs** (Custom House, 50 Anzac Ave., Box 29, Auckland, New Zealand, tel. 09/300–5399, fax 09/359–6730, www.customs.govt.nz).

IN THE U.K.

From countries outside the EU, including Hong Kong, you may bring home, duty-free, 200 cigarettes or 50 cigars; 1 liter of spirits or 2 liters of fortified or sparkling wine or liqueurs; 2 liters of still table wine; 60 ml of perfume; 250 ml of toilet water; plus £136 worth of other goods, including gifts and souvenirs. If returning from outside the EU, prohibited items include meat products, seeds, plants, and fruits.

➤ **INFORMATION: HM Customs and Excise** (Dorset House, Stamford St., Bromley, Kent BR1 1XX, U.K., tel. 020/7202-4227, www.hmce.gov.uk).

IN THE U.S.

U.S. residents who have been out of the country for at least 48 hours (and who have not used the US$400 allowance or any part of it in the past 30 days) may bring home US$400 worth of foreign goods duty-free.

U.S. residents 21 and older may bring back 1 liter of alcohol duty-free. In addition, regardless of your age, you are allowed 200 cigarettes and 100 non-Cuban cigars. Antiques, which the U.S. Customs Service defines as objects more than 100 years old, enter duty-free, as do original works of art done entirely by hand, including paintings, drawings, and sculptures.

You may also mail or ship packages home duty-free: up to US$200 worth of goods for personal use, with a limit of one parcel per addressee per day (except alcohol or tobacco products or perfume worth more than US$5); label the package PERSONAL USE and attach a list of its contents and their retail value. Do not label the package UNSOLICITED GIFT or your duty-free exemption will drop to US$100. Mailed items do not affect your duty-free allowance on your return.

➤ **INFORMATION: U.S. Customs Service** (1300 Pennsylvania Ave. NW, Washington, DC 20229, www.customs.gov; inquiries tel. 202/354-1000; complaints c/o 1300 Pennsylvania Ave. NW, Room

5.4D, Washington, DC 20229; registration of equipment c/o Resource Management, tel. 202/927–0540).

Disabilities & Accessibility

Hong Kong is not the easiest of cities for people in wheelchairs, and few ramps or other provisions for access are provided. However, the airport, City Hall, the Academy for Performing Arts, and the Hong Kong Arts Centre have made efforts to assist people in wheelchairs. For more information, consult the *Hong Kong Access Guide for Disabled Visitors*, available from the Hong Kong Tourism Board (HKTB).

TRANSPORTATION

The airport has moving walkways that transport arriving or departing passengers from the most remote gates in about 70 seconds. Ramps, lifts, and escalators are provided for changes of level. Taxis in Hong Kong do not adapt to special needs of passengers with physical disabilities, but wheelchairs and other walking aids are carried free of charge.

The Mass Transit Railway (MTR), which services Hong Kong and Kowloon and also connects to Tung Chungk and the Chek Lap Kok airport, has ramps or lifts at 19 stations. Ancillary facilities such as tactile guide paths, escalator audible devices, and light emitting diode (LED) display boards are available at most stations.

Electricity

To use electric-powered equipment purchased in the United States or Canada, **bring a converter and adapter.** The electrical current in Hong Kong is 220 volts, 50 cycles alternating current (AC). Some outlets in Hong Kong take plugs with three round prongs, while others use plugs with two square prongs.

If your appliances are dual-voltage, you'll need only an adapter. Don't use 110-volt outlets marked FOR SHAVERS ONLY for high-wattage appliances such as blow-dryers. Most laptops operate equally well on 110 and 220 volts and so require only an adapter.

Emergencies

Most police officers speak some English or will contact someone who does. There are no 24-hour pharmacies, but Fanda Perfume Co., Ltd. and Watson's are usually open until 9 PM.

➤ **EMERGENCY SERVICES: Police, fire, and ambulance** (tel. 999). **Hong Kong Police and Taxi Complaint Hotline** (tel. 2527–7177).

➤ **HOSPITALS: Princess Margaret Hospital** (2–10 Princess Margaret Hospital Rd., Laichikok, Kowloon, tel. 2990–1111). **Queen Elizabeth Hospital** (30 Gascoigne Rd., Kowloon, tel. 2958–8888). **Queen Mary Hospital** (102 Pok Fu Lam Rd., Hong Kong, tel. 2855–3111). **Tang Shiu Kin Hospital** (282 Queen's Rd. E, Hong Kong, tel. 2291–2000).

➤ **PHARMACIES: Fanda Perfume Co., Ltd.** (tel. 2526–6623). **Watson's** (tel. 2915–9065).

English-Language Media

BOOKS

➤ **BOOKSTORES: Bookazines Ltd.** (Pacific House, 20 Queen's Rd., Central, tel. 2521–1649) has a wide selection of books and magazines.

NEWSPAPERS & MAGAZINES

English newspapers printed in Hong Kong include the *South China Morning Post*, *Hong Kong iMail*, the *Asian Wall Street Journal*, the *International Herald Tribune*, and *USA Today International*. The *HK* and the *BC Magazine* are free. The former is an alternative weekly tabloid, the latter a twice-a-month magazine; both provide comprehensive weekly listings.

The *Far Eastern Economic Review* is a Dow Jones publication, and leads the pack for serious, locally produced business publications. *Time* and *Newsweek* both print editions in Hong Kong, joined by the native *Asiaweek* which is part of the Time-Warner family.

RADIO & TELEVISION

There are 13 radio channels, with everything from Cantonese pop music to English news. English-language television channels include ATV World and TVB Pearl. Satellite selections include Star and AUSTV; on cable you can get BBC, CNN, ESPN, and HBO.

Etiquette & Behavior

It won't hurt to **brush up on your use of chopsticks.** Silverware is common in Hong Kong, but it might be seen as a respectful gesture if you try your hand at chopsticks. It is considered proper, when eating rice or soup, to hold the bowl close to your lips and shovel the food into your mouth.

Smoking is common in Hong Kong, but is banned in all indoor public areas.

Hong Kong is extremely crowded; pushing, shoving, and gentle nudges are commonplace. Becoming angry or taking offense to an inadvertent push is considered rude. However, it is not typical of strangers to be excessively touchy-feely with one another. A gregarious hug and boisterous hello will be off-putting to Hong Kongers who don't know you. When you first meet local people, try to **be low-key and subdued,** even if its not in your nature.

BUSINESS ETIQUETTE

Hong Kongers have a keen sense of hierarchy in the office. Egalitarianism may be admired in the United States, but it's often insulting in Hong Kong. **Let the tea lady get the tea and coffee**—that's what she's there for. Your assistant or Chinese colleague is thought to have better things to do than make copies or deliver messages. Hong Kongers are very attached to business cards, so **have plenty of cards available** (printed, if possible, in English on one side and Chinese on the other). Exchange cards by proffering yours with both hands and a slight bow, and receiving one in the same way.

Gay & Lesbian Travel

Criminal sanctions on homosexual relations between consenting adults in Hong Kong were lifted in 1991. Today, Hong Kong has an often not-spoken-about, but hopping gay nightlife. Despite the fact that many local Hong Kongers tend to be intensely xenophobic among themselves (Hong Kongers look down on Shanghainese who look down on Beijingers, etc.), they don't take notice of homosexuals and don't discriminate against them. *Contacts*, a magazine covering the local gay scene, is available for HK$35 at the Fetish Fashion boutique at 32 Cochrane St. in Central (tel. 2544–1155).

Health

FOOD & DRINK

The major health risk for travelers overseas is traveler's diarrhea, caused by eating contaminated fruit or vegetables or drinking contaminated water. Stay away from ice, uncooked food, and unpasteurized milk and milk products. Note, too, that eating raw shellfish has been associated with recent hepatitis outbreaks in Hong Kong. **Drink only bottled water** or water that has been boiled for at least 20 minutes, even when you're brushing your teeth.

OVER-THE-COUNTER REMEDIES

Familiar over-the-counter medications such as aspirin, Tylenol, etc., are available in supermarkets such as Wellcome or even 7-Eleven shops, which are scattered throughout the city. The drugstore chains Fanda Perfume Co., Ltd. and Watson's are located throughout the city.

Holidays

Major holidays in Hong Kong include New Year's (the first weekday in January), Chinese New Year, Easter, Labour Day (May 1), National Day (October 1), and Christmas and Boxing Day (December 25 and 26). There are also numerous Chinese holidays throughout the year.

Language

Hong Kong's official languages are English and Chinese. The most commonly spoken Chinese dialect is Cantonese, but Mandarin—the official language of China, known in Hong Kong as Putonghua—is gaining in popularity. In hotels, major restaurants, stores, and tourist centers, almost everyone speaks English. This is not the case, however, with taxi drivers, bus drivers, and workers in small shops, cafés, and market stalls.

Mail & Shipping

Hong Kong has an excellent reputation for its postal system. Airmail letters to any place in the world should take three to eight days.

➤ **POST OFFICES: Kowloon Central Post Office** (10 Middle Rd., Tsim Sha Tsui). **General Post Office** (2 Connaught Rd., Central).

OVERNIGHT SERVICES

You can find overnight delivery drop-off boxes or offices in most subway stations, malls, and hotels. Call the company for specific locations.

➤ **MAJOR SERVICES: DHL** (tel. 2765–8111). **Federal Express** (tel. 2730–3333). **United Parcel Service** (tel. 2735–3535).

POSTAL RATES

Letters sent from Hong Kong are thought of as going to one of two zones. Zone 1 includes China, Japan, Taiwan, South Korea,

Southeast Asia, Indonesia, and Asia. Zone 2 is everywhere else. International airmail costs HK$2.10 for a letter or postcard weighing under 10 grams mailed to a Zone 1 address, and HK$2.60 for a letter sent to a Zone 2 address. For each additional 10 grams, you will be charged HK$1.10 for Zone 1 and HK$1.20 for Zone 2.

RECEIVING MAIL

The **General Post Office** and **Kowloon Central Post Office** have poste restante counters. Travelers with American Express cards or traveler's checks can receive mail at the **American Express** office (5 Queen's Rd., Central, tel. 2811–6888). Have mail addressed c/o Client Mail Service at this address.

Money Matters

Prices throughout this guide are given for adults. Substantially reduced fees are almost always available for children, students, and senior citizens. For information on taxes, *see* Taxes, *below*.

ATMS

Reliable and safe, ATMs are widely available throughout Hong Kong. If your card was issued from a bank in an English-speaking country, the instructions on the ATM machine will appear in English.

CREDIT CARDS

Throughout this guide, the following abbreviations are used: **AE,** American Express; **DC,** Diners Club; **MC,** MasterCard; and **V,** Visa.

CURRENCY

Units of currency are the Hong Kong dollar ($) and the cent. Bills come in denominations of 1,000, 500, 100, 50, 20, and 10 dollars. Coins are 10, 5, 2, and 1 dollar and 50, 20, and 10 cents. At press time the Hong Kong dollar was fixed at approximately 7.8 dollars to the U.S. dollar, 6.52 to the Canadian dollar, and 12.5 to the pound sterling. The image of Queen Elizabeth II will not appear on new coins, but the old ones are still valid.

CURRENCY EXCHANGE

There are no currency restrictions in Hong Kong. You can exchange currency at the airport, in hotels, in banks, and through private money changers scattered through the tourist areas. For the most favorable rates, **change money at banks.** You'll get better rates from a bank or money changer than from a hotel; just **beware of money changers who advertise "no selling commission"** without mentioning the "buying commission" you must pay when you exchange foreign currency or traveler's checks for Hong Kong dollars. Although ATM transaction fees may be higher abroad than at home, ATM rates are excellent because they are based on wholesale rates offered only by major banks. You won't do as well at exchange booths in airports or rail and bus stations, in hotels, in restaurants, or in stores. To avoid lines at airport exchange booths, **get a bit of local currency before you leave home.**

➤ **EXCHANGE SERVICES: International Currency Express** (tel. 888/278-6628 for orders, www.foreignmoney.com). **Thomas Cook Currency Services** (tel. 800/287-7362 for telephone orders and retail locations, www.us.thomascook.com).

TRAVELER'S CHECKS

Lost or stolen checks can usually be replaced within 24 hours. To ensure a speedy refund, buy your own traveler's checks—don't let someone else pay for them: irregularities like this can cause delays. The person who bought the checks should make the call to request a refund.

Packing

Dress in Hong Kong is generally informal. However, this is a city where suits are still *de rigueur* for meetings. From May through September, Hong Kong's high humidity warrants light clothing; but air-conditioning in hotels and restaurants can be arctic, so bring a sweater or shawl for evening use indoors. Don't forget your swimsuit and sunscreen; several hotels have pools, and you may want to spend some time on one of Hong Kong's many beaches. In October, November, March, and April, a jacket or sweater should suffice, but from December through February bring a raincoat or a light overcoat. At any time of year it's wise to **pack a folding umbrella.**

Check Fodor's *How to Pack* (available in bookstores everywhere) for more tips.

CHECKING LUGGAGE
You are allowed one carry-on bag and one personal article, such as a purse or a laptop computer. Make sure that everything you carry aboard will fit under your seat or in the overhead bin. Get to the gate early, so you can board as soon as possible, before the overhead bins fill up. Airlines flying out of Hong Kong strictly enforce carry-on rules, particularly among holders of economy tickets. Your carry-on bag must not measure more than 9 x 14 x 22 inches, and cannot weigh more than 44 pounds (20 kilograms). Allowances for business-class and first-class passengers are more lenient.

Passports & Visas

When traveling internationally, **carry your passport** even if you don't need one (it's always the best form of I.D.) and **make two photocopies of the data page** (one for someone at home and another for you, carried separately from your passport). If you lose your passport, promptly call the nearest embassy or consulate and the local police.

ENTERING HONG KONG
Citizens of the United Kingdom need only a valid passport to enter Hong Kong for stays of up to six months. Australian, Canadian, New Zealand, and U.S. citizens need only a valid passport to enter Hong Kong for stays up to three months. It is best to have at least six months' validity on your passport before traveling to Asia.

Rest Rooms

Public rest rooms are difficult to find in Hong Kong. Clean, Western-style rest rooms (as opposed to squatters, which are merely holes in the ground) are even more difficult to find. Carry tissues or a toilet-paper roll. Using hotel and restaurant bathrooms is the best bet for a clean environment.

Rickshaws

Because rickshaws are a tourist attraction rather than a common mode of transportation, prices run high. Rates are supposed to be around HK$50 for a five-minute ride, but rickshaw operators are merciless. A posed snapshot can cost almost as much as a ride. **Bargain aggressively and agree on the price in advance.**

Safety

Hong Kong is a relatively safe city day or night. The Hong Kong Police who served under the British government continue to maintain law and order. Avoid carrying large amounts of cash or valuables. Pickpockets are an increasing problem in Hong Kong.

Subway Travel

The four-line Mass Transit Railway (MTR) links Hong Kong Island to Kowloon (the shopping area Tsim Sha Tsui). Trains run frequently and are safe and easy to use. Station entrances are marked with a simple line symbol resembling a man with arms and legs outstretched. You buy tickets from ticket machines; change is available at the stations' Hang Seng Bank counters and from the machines themselves. Fares range from HK$4 to HK$26.

The special Tourist Ticket (HK$25) can save you money. Another bulk-value possibility is the Stored Value Ticket, which also provides access to the aboveground Kowloon–Canton Railway (KCR). Tickets are HK$70, HK$100, and HK$200.

➤ **SUBWAY INFORMATION: HKTB Visitor Hot Line** (tel. 2508–1234). **Mass Transit Railway** (MTR; tel. 2881–8888).

Taxes

Hong Kong levies a 10% service charge and a 3% government tax on hotel rooms. All goods—with the exceptions of alcohol, tobacco, petroleum, perfume, cosmetics, and soft drinks—are duty-free everywhere in Hong Kong.

Taxis

Taxis in Hong Kong and Kowloon are usually red. A taxi's roof sign lights up when the car is available. Fares in urban areas are HK$15 for the first 2 km (1 mi) and HK$1.20 for each additional ⅕ km (⅙₀ mi). There is luggage surcharge of HK$5 per large piece, and surcharges of HK$20 for the Cross-Harbour Tunnel, HK$30 for the Eastern Harbour Tunnel, and HK$45 for the Western Harbour Tunnel. The Tsing Ma Bridge surcharge is HK$30. The Aberdeen, Lion Rock, and Junk Bay tunnels also carry small surcharges (HK$3–HK$8). Taxis cannot pick up passengers where there are double yellow lines. It's hard to find a taxi around 4 PM when the drivers switch shifts.

Many taxi drivers do not speak English, so you may want to **ask someone at your hotel to write out your destination in Chinese. Backseat passengers must wear a seat belt or face a HK$5,000 fine.** Most locals do not tip; however, if you tip HK$5 to HK$10, you're sure to earn yourself a winning smile from your underpaid and overworked taxi driver.

Outside the urban areas, taxis are green. Urban taxis may travel into rural zones, but rural taxis must not cross into urban zones.

There are no interchange facilities for the two, so **do not try to reach an urban area using a green taxi.**

COMPLAINTS
Taxis are usually reliable, but if you have a problem **note the taxi's license number,** which is usually on the dashboard. The complaint hot line is tel. 2577–6866 or 2889–9999.

Telephones

The country code for Hong Kong is 852. When dialing a Hong Kong number from abroad, drop the initial 0 from the local area code. The country code is 1 for the United States and Canada, 61 for Australia, 64 for New Zealand, and 44 for the United Kingdom. The country code for China is 086.

LOCAL CALLS
Your hotel will likely charge you for a local call, so ask a shopkeeper if you can use the phone instead. Most locals will not charge you to you use their phone for a local call since the phone company charges them a flat monthly fee.

Dial 1081 for local directory assistance from English-speaking operators. If a number is constantly busy and you think it might be out of order, call 109 and the operator will check the line. The operators are very helpful if you talk slowly and clearly.

Do not be surprised if you call a local business and they simply hang up on you; often when local, non-native English speakers don't understand you, they simply hang up rather than stammer through a conversation and lose face.

LONG-DISTANCE CALLS
You can dial direct from many hotel and business centers, but always with a hefty surcharge. Dial 013 for international inquiries and for assistance with direct dialing. Dial 10010 for

operator-assisted calls to most countries. Dial 10011 for credit-card, collect, and international conference calls.

You can also make long-distance calls from **Hong Kong Telecom International** (HKTI; Hong Kong Trade Centre, Des Voeux Rd., Central, tel. 2543–0603; TST Hermes House, Kowloon, tel. 2888–7184 or 2888–7185). Here you dial direct from specially marked silver-color phone booths that take phone cards, which are available from HKTI retail shops and 7-Eleven convenience stores. The cards have values of HK$25, HK$50, and HK$100.

LONG-DISTANCE SERVICES

AT&T, MCI, and Sprint access codes make calling long distance relatively convenient, but you may find the local access number blocked in many hotel rooms. First ask the hotel operator to connect you. If the hotel operator balks, ask for an international operator, or dial the international operator yourself. One way to improve your odds of getting connected to your long-distance carrier is to travel with more than one company's calling card (a hotel may block Sprint, for example, but not MCI). If all else fails, call from a pay phone.

➤ **ACCESS CODES: AT&T Direct** (tel. 800/435–0812). **MCI WorldPhone** (tel. 800/444–4141). **Sprint International Access** (tel. 800/877–4646).

PUBLIC PHONES

To make a local call from a pay phone, use a HK$1 coin or, at some phones, a credit card. Pay phones are not hard to find, but locals generally pop into a store and ask to use the phone there, as local calls are free on residence and business lines. Many small stores keep their telephone on the counter facing the street. To make international calls from a pay phone, stop by a 7-Eleven or other convenience store and purchase a prepaid phone card. Multimedia Powerphones have touch screens that allow you to check e-mail and send faxes as well as phone home.

Time

Hong Kong is 12 hours ahead of Eastern Standard Time and 7 hours ahead of Greenwich Mean Time. Remember during daylight savings time to add an hour to the time difference.

Tipping

Hotels and major restaurants usually add a 10% service charge; however, in most cases, this money does not go to the waiters and waitresses. If you want to tip a waiter or waitress, be sure to give it directly to that person and no one else. It is generally not the custom to leave an additional tip in restaurants, taxis, and beauty salons; but it is appreciated. If you buy your newspaper from a corner vendor, consider searching for one of the numerous octogenarians still working for a living—leaving your extra change with these people is another much appreciated tip.

Train Travel

The Kowloon–Canton Railway (KCR) has 13 commuter stops on its 34-km (22-mi) journey through urban Kowloon (from Kowloon to Lo Wu) and the new cities of Shatin and Taipo on its way to the Chinese border. The main station is at Hung Hom, Kowloon, where you can catch express trains to China. Fares range from HK$7.50 to HK$40, and no reservations are required. The KCR meets the MTR at the Kowloon Tong station.

The electronic Octopus Card (HK$100) is accepted on the MTR, Kowloon Canton Railway (KCR), Kowloon Motor Bus (KMB), and Citybus. You can buy the card at ticket offices and HKTB outlets; you place a refundable deposit of HK$50 on it, then reload it with HK$50 or HK$100 increments at Add Value machines or at one of the service counters inside the station.

➤ **TRAIN INFORMATION: HKTB** (The Center, 99 Queen's Rd., Central; Star Ferry Concourse, Kowloon; tel. 2508–1234). **Kowloon–**

Canton Railway (KCR; tel. 2947–7888). **Kowloon Tong station** (tel. 2602–7799).

Trams

STREET TRAMS

Trams run along the north shore of Hong Kong Island from Kennedy Town (in the west) all the way through Central, Wanchai, Causeway Bay, North Point, and Quarry Bay, ending in the former fishing village of Shaukiwan. A branch line turns off in Wanchai toward Happy Valley, where horse races are held in season. Destinations are marked on the front of each tram; the fare is HK$2. **Avoid trams at rush hours,** which are generally 7:30–9 AM and 5–7 PM each weekday. Trams are generally quite slow, and a great way to inhale a lung full of car fumes, but they also give you an opportunity to see the city from a slow-moving vehicle.

PEAK TRAM

Dating from 1888, this railway rises from ground level to Victoria Peak (1,305 ft), offering a panoramic view of Hong Kong. Both residents and tourists use it; most passengers board at the lower terminus between Garden Road and Cotton Tree Drive. (The tram has five stations.) The fare is HK$18 one-way, HK$28 round-trip, and the tram runs every 10–15 minutes daily from 7 AM to midnight. A free shuttle bus runs between the lower terminus and the Star Ferry.

Visitor Information

For round-the-clock phone assistance in Hong Kong, call the multilingual Visitor Hot Line (tel. 2508–1234).

➤ **TOURIST INFORMATION:** Australia: **HKTB** (Level 4, Hong Kong House, 80 Druitt St., Sydney NSW 2000, tel. 612/928–3083, fax 612/929–3383). Canada: **HKTB** (9 Temperance St., 3rd floor, Toronto, Ontario M5H 1Y6, tel. 416/366–2389, fax 416/366–1098). Hong Kong: **HKTB** (Star Ferry Concourse, Kowloon; The Center,

99 Queen's Rd. Central, Central, Hong Kong Island; Hong Kong International Airport). U.K.: **HKTB** (6 Grafton St., London W1X 3LB, tel. 0711/530–7100, fax 020/7/533–7111). U.S.: **HKTB** (590 5th Ave., Suite 590, New York, NY 10036, tel. 212/869–5008, fax 212/730–2605; 610 Enterprise Dr., Suite 200, Oak Brook, IL 60521, tel. 630/575–2828, fax 630/575–2829; 10940 Wilshire Blvd., Suite 1220, Los Angeles, CA 90024, tel. 310/208–4582, fax 310/208–1869).

Web Sites

Do check out the World Wide Web when you're planning your trip. You'll find everything from weather forecasts to virtual tours of famous cities. Be sure to **visit Fodors.com** (www.fodors.com), a complete travel planning site.

For a comprehensive guide to what's happening in Hong Kong, check out the HKTB's excellent site, www.discoverhongkong.com. For the latest political information plus news and interesting business links try the official Hong Kong government site at www.info.gov.hk. Hong Kong iMail Newspaper's site at www.hk-imail.com has the day's news and a look at what's happening in Hong Kong and the region.

When to Go

During Hong Kong's high season, October through late December, the weather is pleasant, with sunny days and cool, comfortable nights. January, February, and sometimes early March are cold and dank, with long periods of overcast skies and rain. March and April can be either cold and miserable or sunny and beautiful. By May the temperature is consistently warm and comfortable.

J⎯ ⎯h September is typhoon season, when the weather is hot, sticky, and very rainy. Typhoons (called hurricanes in the Atlantic) must be treated with respect, and Hong Kong is prepared for these blustery assaults; if a storm is approaching, the airwaves will crackle with information, and your hotel and various public institutions will post the appropriate signals. When a No. 8 signal is posted, Hong Kong closes down completely. Head immediately for your hotel and stay put. This is serious business—bamboo scaffolding can come hurtling through the streets like spears, ships can be sunk in the harbor, and large areas of the territory are often flooded.

➤ **FORECASTS: Weather Channel Connection** (tel. 900/932-8437), 95¢ per minute from a Touch-Tone phone.

CLIMATE

The following are average daily maximum and minimum temperatures for Hong Kong.

Jan.	64F	18C	May	82F	28C	Sept.	85F	29C
	56	13		74	23		77	25
Feb.	63F	17C	June	85F	29C	Oct.	81F	27C
	55	13		78	26		73	23
Mar.	67F	19C	July	87F	31C	Nov.	74F	23C
	60	16		78	26		65	18
Apr.	75F	24C	Aug.	87F	31C	Dec.	68F	20C
	67	19		78	26		59	15

index

ICONS AND SYMBOLS

★ Our special recommendations
⑤ Good for kids (rubber duck)
③ ❸ Numbers in white and black circles that appear on the maps, in the margins, and within the tours correspond to one another.

A

Aberdeen, 29–30, 54
Academy for Performing Arts, 23
Admiralty, 47, 49, 65, 103, 106
Admiralty Complex, 67–68
American Peking Restaurant, 50
Amusement parks, 31
Antiques shops, 72–74
Apleichau (Duck's Tongue) Island, 30
Art galleries and museums, 23, 31, 33, 35, 74–75
Arts, 96–99
Auction houses, 75
Aw Boon Haw (Tiger Balm) Gardens, 27

B

Bank of China, 13–14
Bars, 91–92
Bazaars, 71–72
Best Noodle Restaurant, 60
Bird Garden, 33
Bishop Lei International House, 106
Blue (restaurant), 44
Boathouse (restaurant), 55
Bonham Strand East and West, 14
Booth Lodge, 120
BP International House, 115

C

Cafe Deco Bar and Grill, 50
Camera equipment, 75–76
Canton Road, 37
Cargo Handling Basin, 27
Caritas Bianchi Lodge, 120
Carpet and rug shops, 76
Cat Street, 20
Causeway Bay, 26–29, 53–54, 65–66, 108–109
Causeway Bay Typhoon Shelter, 27
Cenotaph, 18

Central and Western Districts, 9–21, 40–41, 44–46, 63–64, 102
Central Plaza, 26
Century (hotel), 107
Century Inn North Point, 109–110
Ceramics shops, 76–77
Children's attractions, 21–22, 23, 27, 31, 33, 35, 36
China Lan Kwai Fong (restaurant), 40
China Products Company, 69
Chinese Arts & Crafts, 69
Chinese gifts, 77
Chinese opera, 97
Chinese Resources Center, 69
Chung Kiu Chinese Products Emporium, 70
Chung Thai Food Restaurant and Sea Food, 57, 59
Churches, 22
Cityplaza, 68
Clothing factory outlets, 78–81
Clothing shops, 77–78
Cocktail bars, 92–93
Computer shops, 81
Concourse (hotel), 118
Conrad International (hotel), 103
Credit cards, 137

D

Dance, 97
Dan Ryan's (restaurant), 47
Deep Water Bay, 30
Department stores, 69–71
Des Voeux Road West, 14
Dim Sum, 51
Dim Sum (restaurant), 53
Dining
Hong Kong Island, 40–56
Kowloon, 57–61
price categories, 39
Discos, 93–94
Dorsett Seaview (hotel), 119
Dumpling Shop, 50

E

Eating Plus (restaurant), 46
Eaton (hotel), 118
El Cid (restaurant), 56
Electronics shops, 81–82
El Pomposo (restaurant), 44
Emperor Happy Valley (hotel), 109
Eu Yan Sang Medical Hall, 19
Excelsior (hotel), 108–109

F

Fat Angelo's (restaurant), 53
Felix (restaurant), 60
Festival Walk, 68
Film, 98
Flower Market, 71
Folk clubs, 98
Forum (restaurant), 53
Fung Ping Shan Museum, 31
Furniture shops, 82–83

G

Gaddi's (restaurant), 60
Gardens, 23, 27
Garden View International House, 106
Golden Orchid Thai Restaurant, 57
Good Luck Thai (restaurant), 46
Government House, 21
Grand Cafe, 51–52
Grand Hyatt (hotel), 106–107
Grand Plaza (hotel), 110
Grand Stanford Inter-Continental (hotel), 117
Grappa's (restaurant), 49
Great Shanghai Restaurant, 59
Grissini (restaurant), 52

H

Handicraft shops, 83–84
Happy Garden (restaurant), 56
Happy Garden Noodle & Congee Kitchen, 59
Happy Valley, 26–29, 109
Happy Valley Racetrack, 27–28
Harbour City, 68–69
Harbour Plaza (hotel), 110, 112
Harbour View International House, 107–108
Holiday Inn Golden Mile, 113
Hollywood Road, 14
Holy Carpenter Guest House, 112

Hongkong & Shanghai Bank (HSBC), 15
Hong Kong Arts Centre, 23
Hong Kong Convention and Exhibition Centre, 26
Hong Kong Cultural Centre, 33
Hong Kong Island
dining, 40–56
exploring, 9–32
lodging, 102–110
shopping, 63–66, 67–68
Hong Kong Museum of Art, 33, 35
Hong Kong Museum of History, 35
Hong Kong Park, 21–22
Hong Kong Science Museum, 35
Hong Kong Space Museum, 35
Hong Kong University, 30–31
Hong Kong Yacht Club, 28
Horse racing, 27–28
Hostess clubs, 94
Hotels. ☞ See Lodging
Hunan Garden (restaurant), 41
Hung Hom, 67, 110, 148

I

Icons and symbols, 148
Indochine 1929 (restaurant), 46
Inter-Continental Hong Kong (hotel), 112
Island Seafood & Oyster Bar, 54
Island Shangri-La (hotel), 103

J

Jade market, 35, 71
Jamia Masjid and Islamic Centre, 36
Jamia Mosque, 15
Jardine House, 15
Jaspa's (restaurant), 57
Jazz clubs, 98
Jewelry shops, 84–85
Jimmy's Kitchen, 44–45
Joyce Boutique, 70
Jumbo Floating Restaurant, 54
J. W. Marriott (hotel), 103, 106

K

Kansu Street Jade Market, 35, 71
Kath+Man+Du (restaurant), 45
Kimberley (hotel), 115
Kowloon
dining, 57–61
exploring, 32–37
lodging, 110–120
shopping, 66–67, 68–69
Kowloon (hotel), 115
Kowloon Park, 36
Kowloon Shangri-La (hotel), 117
Kung Tak Lam (restaurant), 61
Kwun Yum Temple, 28

L

Ladies' Market, 71
Landmark area, 15, 68
Lane Crawford (department store), 70
Leather goods shops, 86
Legislative Council Building, 18
Lei Cheng Uk Museum, 36
Linen shops, 86
Lobster Bar, 49
Lo Chiu Vietnamese Restaurant, 61
Lodging, 101
Hong Kong Island, 102–110
Kowloon, 110–120
price categories, 102
Lucy's (restaurant), 55
Luk Kwok (hotel), 107

M

Majestic (hotel), 119
Mak's Noodles Limited, 41
Mandarin Grill, 41, 44
Mandarin Oriental (hotel), 102
Man Mo Temple, 18
Man Wah (restaurant), 40
Marco Polo hotels
Gateway, 113–114
Hongkong, 113
Prince, 114
Markets, 71–72
Marks & Spencer (department store), 70
Martial arts supplies, 86–87
M at the Fringe (restaurant), 44
Meal plans, 101
Metropole (hotel), 119
Middle Kingdom, 31
Midlevels Escalator, 18
Miramar (hotel), 114
Mistral (restaurant), 60–61
Mong Kok, 67, 118–120
Mosques, 15, 36
Museum of Tea Ware, 21–22
Museums. ☞ *Also* Art galleries and museums, 21–22, 35, 36
Music, 98

N

Nathan Road, 36
Nepal (restaurant), 45
New Astor (hotel), 115–116
New Cathay (hotel), 109
Newton (hotel), 110
New World Renaissance (hotel), 114
New World Shopping Centre, 69
Nice Fragrance Vegetarian Kitchen, 52
Nicholini's (restaurant), 49
Nightclubs, 93–94
Nightlife, 91–95
Nikko (hotel), 117
Ning Po Street, 37
Noonday Gun, 28–29
North Point, 26–29, 109–110

O

Ocean Park, 31
Open Kitchen, 52

P

Pao Gallery, 23
Park Lane (hotel), 109
Parks, 21–22, 29, 32, 36
Pavilion (restaurant), 44
Peak area, 21–23, 50
Peak Outlook (restaurant), 50
Peak Tower, 22
Peak Tram, 22

Peninsula Hotel, 36, 112
Performing arts centers, 96–97
Petrus (restaurant), 47
Piano bars, 92–93
Price categories
dining, 39
lodging, 102
Pruton Prudential (hotel), 119
Pubs, 94–95

Q

Quarry Bay, 110
Queen's Road Central, 19
Queen's Road East, 26

R

Ramada Hotel Kowloon, 115
Regal Hongkong Hotel, 108
Regal Kowloon (hotel), 118
Renaissance Harbour View (hotel), 107
Repulse Bay, 31, 54–55
Restaurants. ☞ See Dining
Ritz-Carlton (hotel), 102
Royal Garden (hotel), 117–118
Royal Pacific Hotel & Towers, 116
Royal Plaza (hotel), 119–120

S

Saigon Beach (restaurant), 52
Sai Kung, 57, 59
St. John's Cathedral, 22
Salisbury YMCA, 116

Seibu (department store), 71
Shamrock (hotel), 120
Shanghai Shanghai (restaurant), 41
Shanghai Street, 37
Shanghai Tang Department Store, 70
Shek O, 32, 56
Shek O Chinese and Thailand Seafood Restaurant, 56
Sheraton Hong Kong Hotel and Towers, 113
Shoe shops, 87
Shopping, 63
centers and malls, 67–69
department stores, 69–71
major shopping areas, 63–67
markets and bazaars, 71–72
specialty shopping, 72–88
Sichuan Garden (restaurant), 41
Sincere (department store), 71
SoHo, 18, 40–41, 44–46
SoHo SoHo (restaurant), 40
South Side, 29–32
Spices (restaurant), 55
Spring Moon (restaurant), 59
Stanley, 32, 55–56, 66
Stanley's French Restaurant, 55
Stanley Village Market, 71–72
Star Ferry Pier, 37
Star Ferry Terminal, 19
Statue Square, 19

Staunton Street, 18
Steam and Stew Inn, 51
Symbols and icons, 148

T

Tai Tau Chau, 32
Tai Wong Temple, 26
T'ang Court (restaurant), 59
Tea shops, 87–89
Temples, 18, 26, 28, 29, 30, 37
Temple Street, 37
Temple Street Night Market, 72
Thai Basil (restaurant), 49
Thai Lemongrass (restaurant), 46
Theater, 99
Times Square, 68
Tin Hau temples, 29, 30, 37
Tokio Joe (restaurant), 45
Toscana (restaurant), 45
Tott's Asian Grill & Bar, 53
Tsim Sha Tsui, 59–61, 66–67, 112–118
Tso Choi Koon (restaurant), 57

U

Upper Lascar Row, 20

V

Verandah (restaurant), 54
Victoria Clock Tower, 37
Victoria Park, 29
Victoria Peak, 22
Vong (restaurant), 44

W

Wanchai, 23–26, 50–52, 65, 106–108
Watch shops, 88
Web sites, TK
Wesley (hotel), 108
Western Market, 20
Windsor (hotel), 116
Wine bars, 95
Wing Lok Street, 20
Wong Tai Sin Temple, 37
W's Entrecote (restaurant), 54
Wu Kong (restaurant), 60
Wyndham Street, 20–21

Y

Yau Ma Tei, 67, 118–120
Ye Shanghai (restaurant), 47
Yü (restaurant), 61
Yue Hwa Chinese Products Emporium, 70
Yung Kee (restaurant), 40

Z

Zen (restaurant), 47
Zoological and Botanical Gardens, 23

FODOR'S POCKET HONG KONG

EDITORS: Shannon Kelly, Melissa Klurman

Editorial Contributors: Denise Cheung, Eva Chui, Tobias Parker, Lara Wozniak

Editorial Production: Tom Holton

Maps: David Lindroth, *cartographer*; Rebecca Baer, Bob Blake *map editors*

Design: Fabrizio La Rocca, *creative director*; Tigist Getachew, *art director*; Melanie Marin, *photo editor*

Production/Manufacturing: Angela L. McLean

Cover Photograph: Walter Bibikow/ Age Fotostock

COPYRIGHT

Copyright © 2002 by Fodors LLC

Fodor's is a registered trademark of Random House, Inc.

All rights reserved under International and Pan-American Copyright Conventions. Published in the United States by Fodor's Travel Publications, a unit of Fodors LLC, a subsidiary of Random House, Inc., and simultaneously in Canada by Random House of Canada Limited, Toronto. Distributed by Random House, Inc., New York.

No maps, illustrations, or other portions of this book may be reproduced in any form without written permission from the publisher.

First Edition

ISBN 0-676-90222-7

ISSN 1537-5595

SPECIAL SALES

Fodor's Travel Publications are available at special discounts for bulk purchases for sales promotions or premiums. Special editions, including personalized covers, excerpts of existing guides, and corporate imprints, can be created in large quantities for special needs. For more information, contact your local bookseller or write to Special Markets, Fodor's Travel Publications, 280 Park Avenue, New York, NY 10017. Inquiries from Canada should be directed to your local Canadian bookseller or sent to Random House of Canada, Ltd., Marketing Department, 2775 Matheson Boulevard East, Mississauga, Ontario L4W 4P7. Inquiries from the United Kingdom should be sent to Fodor's Travel Publications, 20 Vauxhall Bridge Road, London SW1V 2SA, England.

PRINTED IN THE UNITED STATES OF AMERICA

10 9 8 7 6 5 4 3 2 1

IMPORTANT TIP

Although all prices, opening times, and other details in this book are based on information supplied to us at press time, changes occur all the time in the travel world, and Fodor's cannot accept responsibility for facts that become outdated or for inadvertent errors or omissions. So **always confirm information when it matters,** especially if you're making a detour to visit a specific place.